Hearing God
When You Hurt

Hearing God When You Hurt

James Montgomery Boice

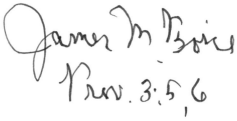

James M Boice
Prov. 3:5,6

Baker Books

A Division of Baker Book House Co
Grand Rapids, Michigan 49516

Published by Baker Books
a division of Baker Book House Company
P.O. Box 6287, Grand Rapids, MI 49516–6287

Printed in the United States of America

Library of Congress Cataloging-in-Publication Data

Boice, James Montgomery, 1938–
  Hearing God when you hurt / James Montgomery Boice.
    p.   cm.
  Includes bibliographical references.
  ISBN 0–8010–5229–7 (pbk.)
    1. Suffering—Biblical teaching. 2. Bible O.T. Psalms LII–LXIII—Criticism,
interpretation, etc. 3. David, King of Israel. 4. Consolation. 5. Saul, King of
Israel. 6. Persecution—Biblical teaching. I. Title.
BS1430.6.S8B65   1995
223'.206—dc20   95–24328

To GOD
who saves me
who hears my voice

Contents

Preface

To many people the psalms probably seem to be put together in a somewhat random fashion, but that is not the case. Many are linked by common themes, and there are also important subgroupings within the larger Psalter. The "psalms of ascent" (Psalms 120–134) are one obvious example. They were sung by devout pilgrims as they made their way up to Jerusalem for one of the yearly feasts. The "psalms of praise" that come toward the end of the whole collection of psalms are another example.

Midway through the second book of psalms is the collection that is the basis for this study: Psalms 52–63. These psalms were written by David, and most are linked by their titles to that dark period of his life when he was fleeing from his powerful and relentless enemy, King Saul. These psalms have titles like "When Doeg the Edomite had gone to Saul and told him: 'David has gone to the house of Ahimelech'"; "When the Ziphites had gone to Saul and said, 'Is not David hiding among us?'"; "When the Philistines had seized him in Gath"; "When he had fled from Saul into the cave"; "When Saul had sent men to watch David's house in order to kill him"; "When he fought Aram Naharaim and Aram Zobah, and when Joab returned and struck down twelve thousand Edomites in the Valley of Salt"; and "When he was in the Desert of Judah." Not all of these psalms have titles, but they all belong to dark periods of acute distress and danger.

9

What we need to see is how David sought God passionately in such times.

The reason for studying these psalms together and carefully is that we also go through times in which we are in genuine peril from people who despise or hate us and times when our minds are troubled and our souls are in anguish. What should we do in such times? Where should we turn? Who will help us?

These psalms tell us that we must do what David did—turn to God. If others are against us, God at least is for us and is listening to hear our cries and will carry us through the dark times. What is more, he will speak through his Word to provide both teaching and comfort. In Psalm 55:16–17, David says:

> I call to God,
>   and the LORD saves me.
> Evening, morning and noon
>   I cry out in distress,
>   and he hears my voice.

God hears us. But the question is, Do we hear him? Do we pause long enough and listen well enough to hear what he has to say for our comfort?

As we go through these important psalms together, I trust you will hear your cries echoed in David's own and, more important, that you will hear God speak to you through David. God is the same as he ever was, and David's comfort can be your comfort too. May "the LORD bless you and keep you; the LORD make his face shine upon you and be gracious to you; the LORD turn his face toward you and give you peace" (Num. 6:24–26).

Psalm
52

Why do you boast of evil, you mighty man?
  Why do you boast all day long,
  you who are a disgrace in the eyes of God?
Your tongue plots destruction;
  it is like a sharpened razor,
  you who practice deceit.
You who love evil rather than good,
  falsehood rather than speaking the truth.   *Selah*
You love every harmful word,
  O you deceitful tongue!

Surely God will bring you down to everlasting ruin:
  He will snatch you up and tear you from your tent;
  he will uproot you from the land of the living. *Selah*

The righteous will see and fear;
  they will laugh at him, saying,
"Here now is the man
  who did not make God his stronghold
  but trusted in his great wealth
  and grew strong by destroying others!"

But I am like an olive tree
    flourishing in the house of God;
I trust in God's unfailing love
    for ever and ever.
I will praise you forever for what you have done;
    in your name I will hope, for your name is good.
    I will praise you in the presence of your saints.

Righteous Judgment for a Wicked Man

*I*f I were to tell you about a man who was driven from his home because soldiers were lying in wait to kill him, was betrayed by friends who had been close to him, and was pursued from place to place like a fugitive, you might think I was describing a man who had done some terrible wrong or had been abandoned by God. But I am not. I am describing a dark period in the life of Israel's great King David before he became king. During this time as well as later he was a favored child of God. In fact, he was called "a man after [God's] own heart" (1 Sam. 13:14). This was indeed a dark period, but God used it to mature David's already outstanding character, and he also kept and preserved him through it.

This will be the case with you, if you are going through hard times and are a Christian. Dark days do not mean that you have displeased God or that God has abandoned you, though we tend to imagine that. God is with us even in the worst circumstances, and he will bring us through them triumphantly. What is important is that we learn to go through them as David did, that is, by drawing close to God, listening to what he has to say, and asking him to do with us as seems best to him.

The heading for Psalm 52 gives the context as one of the most bitter experiences in the life of David: "When Doeg the Edomite had gone to Saul and told him: 'David has gone to the house of Ahimelech.'"

As a result of this report and at Saul's command, eighty-five of the priests of a town called Nob together with their wives, children, and the citizens of Nob were killed by Doeg. David's two responses to this tragic massacre are recorded in 1 Samuel 22:22–23 and in Psalm 52. In the 1 Samuel passage, David recognizes and confesses his own unwitting responsibility for the massacre. In Psalm 52 he documents the deliberate wickedness of Doeg, the "mighty man" of verse 1 who boasts of evil.

David and Ahimelech

But first the story. David had been forced to flee Jerusalem after his sad parting with Jonathan in the field outside the city, and he had come to Nob, one of the cities of the priests. David presented himself to Ahimelech, the chief priest, asking for help. Ahimelech must have suspected that something was wrong because David had come unarmed and alone, without his customary band of soldiers. We are told that Ahimelech trembled when he saw David. But David lied to him, saying that Saul had sent him on a secret errand and that he had arranged to meet his soldiers later. Then he asked for food and was given the consecrated bread that had been on the Table of Shewbread, presented to the Lord. Because David had no weapon, Ahimelech also gave him the sword of Goliath, which had been kept in the sanctuary and was the only weapon available. In the midst of the story we find this solemn notation: "Now one of Saul's servants was there that day, detained before the LORD; he was Doeg the Edomite, Saul's head shepherd" (1 Sam. 21:7).

In chapter 22 the scene shifts to a hillside at Gibeah, where King Saul was assembled with his officials and personal military guard. The king was feeling sorry for himself because he had heard that David was gathering supporters in Judah; he knew that Jonathan was David's friend and had made a covenant of friendship with him, and no one was telling him what was going on.

Sadly, Doeg was present, and seeing this as an opportunity to gain favor with the king, he volunteered, "I saw the son of Jesse come to Ahimelech son of Ahitub at Nob. Ahimelech inquired of the LORD for him; he also gave him provisions and the sword of Goliath the Philistine" (1 Sam. 22:9–10). This infuriated Saul. He called for Ahimelech and accused him of conspiracy. Ahimelech replied that no one in the kingdom was more loyal to Saul than David. Besides, how was he to know there was a problem between David and the king? When David came to Nob, he assisted David just as he had done many times previously and would expect to do always.

Saul was irrational. "You will surely die, Ahimelech, you and your father's whole family," he said (v. 16). But, when Saul ordered his guards to kill God's priests they refused, considering it sacrilege to lift a hand against the anointed servants of the Lord.

Saul then ordered Doeg to do it. "So Doeg the Edomite turned and struck them down. That day he killed eighty-five men who wore the linen ephod. He also put to the sword Nob, the town of the priests, with its men and women, its children and infants, and its cattle, donkeys and sheep" (vv. 18–19). One man, Abiathar, a son of Ahimelech, escaped and fled to David. To him David confessed his own unwitting part in this tragedy: "That day, when Doeg the Edomite was there, I knew he would be sure to tell Saul. I am responsible for the death of your father's whole family" (v. 22).

That is the story. It is told in these two chapters of 1 Samuel and is never mentioned again anywhere else in the Bible, except in the title of Psalm 52. This psalm is David's personal evaluation of Doeg and the tragic events he precipitated. It has three parts: (1) a description of Doeg's wickedness (vv. 1–4), (2) the prophesied end of this exceedingly evil man (vv. 5–7), and (3) a final contrasting portrait of David himself, showing what he was and what he hoped always to do and continue being (vv. 8–9).

Portrait of a Very Wicked Man

As we read the first stanza of this psalm we find Doeg's evil character described in three aspects.

1. *Doeg was proud.* The word used in the psalm is *boast,* and it occurs twice, both times in verse 1: "Why do you boast of evil, you mighty man? Why do you boast all day long?" The thought conveyed in this Hebrew word is not necessarily that of a person strutting around making extravagant claims about his abilities but rather of a smug self-sufficiency that is so convinced of its superiority that it does not parade itself openly. Sometimes outward boasting is a cover-up for a person's inner insecurities, but that was not what Doeg was like. As the British scholar Derek Kidner wrote, "The real point is the man's self-satisfaction. He thinks himself clever, he is absorbed in his intrigues."[1]

There is some evidence for this evil element of Doeg's character in the story. If we read it carefully, we notice that there was a considerable time gap between the day Doeg was in Nob and saw David and when he reported this fact to King Saul. The end of 1 Samuel 21 tells of David's escape to Achish, one of the rulers of the Philistines, and the start of the next chapter tells of David gathering his mighty men about him while in the stronghold at Adullam. Both of these events intervene between the time Doeg saw David with Ahimelech in Nob and when he reported this to Saul. So it was not a case of the Edomite's merely blurting out what he knew at the first opportunity. On the contrary, he knew he had a piece of valuable information and kept it to himself until a time that would best serve his interests. He saw his opportunity when Saul complained that not one of his retainers was concerned about him or told him anything.

2. *Doeg loved evil.* Verse 3 says, "You love evil rather than good, falsehood rather than speaking the truth." The fact that Doeg told Saul what he knew is not proof of his love of evil. He might simply have been trying to advance himself with Saul. But his ruthless murder of the priests of Nob and their families showed that he actually hated all who stood for righteousness—Ahimelech stood for righteousness and had spoken truthfully when he was interrogated by Saul—and Doeg wanted to eliminate such people and thus advance and align himself with the most evil aspects of Saul's deteriorating moral character.

3. *Doeg used words as his weapon.* At first glance this may not seem so bad. In fact, it seems out of place. We know that boasting is bad, and loving evil is bad by definition. But words seem relatively harmless. Yet when we look carefully at the stanza we see that this is the vice most emphasized.

> Your tongue plots destruction;
>   it is like a sharpened razor,
>   you who practice deceit.
> You love evil rather than good,
>   falsehood rather than speaking the truth.
> You love every harmful word,
>   O you deceitful tongue!
>
> verses 2–4

~ **Psalm 52** ~

This tells us something about the nature of falsehood, deceit, and lies as well as the potentially murderous effects of words. It teaches that words are not morally neutral. They are a powerful force either for evil or good. The statements of the psalm do something else too. They bring this denunciation of Doeg's character closer to ourselves and warn us of the evil of which we are capable.

Believers in Jesus Christ should not be people who love evil. In fact, people who love evil rather than good are not Christians. Christians should not be self-satisfied, clever, or absorbed in their own intrigues. But what about our words? Do we fail to tell the truth or even engage in deceit? These may be more common sins, but loose talk or less than honest and upright conversation should not be found in a Christian.

If this were not a danger for us, why would James have written about the harm the tongue can do in that extensive treatment found in chapter 3?

> The tongue is a small part of the body, but it makes great boasts. Consider what a great forest is set on fire by a small spark. The tongue also is a fire, a world of evil among the parts of the body. It corrupts the whole person, sets the whole course of his life on fire, and is itself set on fire by hell.
>
> All kinds of animals, birds, reptiles and creatures of the sea are being tamed and have been tamed by man, but no man can tame the tongue. It is a restless evil, full of deadly poison.
>
> With the tongue we praise our Lord and Father, and with it we curse men, who have been made in God's likeness. Out of the same mouth come praise and cursing. My brothers, this should not be.
>
> James 3:5–10

The whole passage is sobering, but especially those last words: "Brothers, this should not be." "Brothers" means Christians. So this is a statement that believers in Christ are sometimes guilty of the same vice seen in wicked Doeg and do corresponding harm.

In England during World War II a war poster was displayed all over the country as a warning against unwitting disclosure of troop movements or other military secrets. It contained the words: "Loose talk costs lives." That is true spiritually as well. So instead of being people whose talk is undisciplined or loose, we should be people whose conversation is constructive and—above all—truthful.

When I say grace before meals, one of the prayers I frequently make is that God will "guide our conversation." It is a prayer we might all pray at all times and on all occasions.

A Prophesied Judgment

Having described Doeg's evil character, David next prophesies his end. It is an important principle in the psalms, often stated by David but also by others, that in a moral universe ultimately evil does not prosper but is instead brought down. And by contrast, the righteous excel.

This is not to be taken as a truth with no exceptions, of course, for clearly the righteous sometimes do suffer, even death. After all, Ahimelech and the other priests as well as their families were killed by Doeg—that is the occasion of this psalm. And the wicked sometimes flourish. That is one of the things that bothers the psalm writers. They can't understand why evil people frequently do prosper or why the judgment of God on such persons is often long delayed. The psalm writers were not naïve. In fact, they were far more sensitive to these anomalies than we often are. But underlying these observations and more basic was their steadfast conviction that in the end the wicked are brought down and the righteous are preserved and blessed by God.

The second stanza contains two main ideas: first, what God will do to Doeg eventually, and second, what the righteous will do when at last they witness God's judgment.

The statement of God's judgment on Doeg contains four vigorous verbs meant to stress the utter totality of his ruin. The first verb is *bring down*. It has the idea of tearing something down in order to break it into pieces, as when an altar is torn down and demolished. The second verb is *snatch up*. It has the additional thought of twisting something up or out, as trees are sometimes torn out of the ground by twisting them. The third verb is *tear* (or *sweep*) *away*. The New International Version reads "tear you from your tent," but other scholars believe the idea is actually "so you may no longer be a tent," meaning a family in Israel. As Doeg had destroyed the families of the priests, so he and his family would be expunged from Israel. The final verb, *uproot* (or *eradicate*), reinforces this idea.

At this point we might expect something about punishment in the life to come, judgment of the soul as well as of the body. But instead we find two verses describing what the righteous will do when they witness God's judgment on the evil man. They will "see" it and "fear" (v. 6). That is, they will stand in awe of God's mighty judging acts. And they will "laugh," drawing the appropriate conclusion on Doeg's folly in pursuing evil rather than good and falsehood rather than truth.

> They will laugh at him, saying,
> "Here now is the man
>   who did not make God his stronghold
> but trusted in his great wealth
>   and grew strong by destroying others!"
> verses 6–7

⌖ Psalm 52 ⌖

It is the lesson drawn from God's judgment that keeps the laughter of the righteous from being mere selfish delight at the fall of some mighty enemy. This is not mockery at another person's misfortune. It is satisfaction at the rightness of things when God intervenes to judge those who have done great harm to others.

A Contrasting Portrait of the Righteous

We have to be careful at this point, of course, because we are sinners too, and it is fatally easy for us to forget our own evil when we see how others are brought down. In fact, we often find improper satisfaction in others' failures. I believe this is why we have the third, final stanza, in which David suggests what the proper attitude of the righteous should be, using himself as an example:

> But I am like an olive tree
>   flourishing in the house of God;
> I trust in God's unfailing love
>   for ever and ever.
> I will praise you forever for what you have done;
>   in your name I will hope, for your name is good.
>   I will praise you in the presence of your saints.
>   verses 8–9

We know from the story of David's later life that he did not always live up to a righteous standard. But at the time he wrote this he could honestly say that he was "like an olive tree flourishing in the house of God." The olive is one of the most lasting of all trees. With its dark, waxen leaves it survives even the worst summer droughts, and it is valuable in its ability to produce a yearly crop of olives.

〜 **Psalm 52** 〜

At this point it is difficult not to think back to Psalm 1, of which Psalm 52 is a specific illustration. Psalm 1 contrasted the way of the righteous with the way of the wicked, showing the righteous person to be "like a tree planted by streams of water, which yields its fruit in season and whose leaf does not wither" (v. 3), while the wicked are described as "chaff that the wind blows away" (v. 4). "Therefore," says the psalmist:

> The wicked will not stand in the judgment,
>   nor sinners in the assembly of the righteous.
>
> For the LORD watches over the way of the righteous,
>   but the way of the wicked will perish.
>   verses 5–6

Assuming the prophecy of Doeg's eventual end to have been fulfilled, the ways of David and Doeg illustrate that teaching.

Do you and I believe that? Do we believe that God really is in control of this world and that evil will be judged and righteousness will be rewarded in the end, even if not openly in every case right now? If we do, then the last verse of Psalm 52 describes what we will do and be like. In it David does three things. First, *he praises God* ("I will praise you forever for what you have done," v. 9). Second, *he trusts God for the future* ("I trust in God's unfailing love for ever and ever" and "in your name I will hope, for your name is good," vv. 8–9). Third, *he bears witness of these truths before others* ("I will praise you in the presence of your saints," v. 9).

Charles Haddon Spurgeon wrote, "Before or among the saints David intended to wait, feeling it to be good both for him and them to look to the Lord alone, and wait for the manifestation of his character in due season. Men must not too much fluster us; our strength is to sit still. Let the mighty ones boast, we will wait on the Lord; and if their haste brings them present honor, our patience will have its turn by-and-by, and bring us the honor which excelleth."[2] That is true. It will surely happen. The honor of God stands behind such an outcome. But when it does happen, make sure you are faithful in telling others about it, as David did.

Psalm 53

The fool says in his heart,
    "There is no God."
They are corrupt, and their ways are vile;
    there is no one who does good.

God looks down from heaven
    on the sons of men
to see if there are any who understand,
    any who seek God.
Everyone has turned away,
    they have together become corrupt;
there is no one who does good,
    not even one.

Will the evildoers never learn—
    those who devour my people as men eat bread
    and who do not call on God?
There they were, overwhelmed with dread,
    where there was nothing to dread.
God scattered the bones of those who attacked you;
    you put them to shame, for God despised them.

Oh, that salvation for Israel would come out of
        Zion!
    When God restores the fortunes of his people,
    let Jacob rejoice and Israel be glad!

A Psalm That Is Repeated

$\mathcal{P}$salm 53 is a near repetition of a psalm that has already occurred in the Psalter, Psalm 14. That is, Psalm 14 appears again as Psalm 53, except for a few minor changes and the addition of the last three lines of verse 5. Moreover, in addition to Psalms 14 and 53 being almost identical, the most important part of these psalms (vv. 1–3) is also repeated in Romans 3:10–12. Anything God says once demands attention. Anything he says twice demands our most intent attention. What about something he says three times, as he does in this case? A case like this demands our keenest concentration, contemplation, assimilation, and even memorization. These are words that, to use the often quoted phrase of the collect from the *Book of Common Prayer,* we ought to "read, mark, learn, and inwardly digest."

This psalm is repeated because God knows we have much to learn from it. If we have not learned all we can from studying Psalm 14, we need to turn to it a second time, as Psalm 53, to see what new lessons it has for our spiritual growth and blessing.

Spurgeon thought that we profit from it more as we grow older. He wrote, "All repetitions are not vain repetitions.

We are slow to learn, and need line upon line." Assuming that Psalm 53 was written by David late in life and that he had written Psalm 14 earlier, Spurgeon said, "David after a long life, found men no better than they were in his youth. Holy Writ never repeats itself needlessly, [therefore] there is good cause for the second copy of this Psalm." Making a point by the numbering of the psalms, he noted, "If our age has advanced from fourteen to fifty-three, we shall find the doctrine of this psalm more evident than in our youth."[1]

Slight Differences

There are a few differences between Psalms 14 and 53, however, so we should start by noting them. Most are slight. For example, in verse 1, the word *deeds* in Psalm 14 is changed to *ways* in Psalm 53. In verse 3, "All have turned aside" is changed to "everyone has turned away." In verse 4, "*the* evil-doers" replaces "evildoers." The only apparent effect of these minor changes is to intensify or heighten the sentiments slightly.

A change that is a bit more significant is the replacing of the name Jehovah (LORD) with Elohim ("God") throughout Psalm 53. Each psalm refers to God seven times, but in Psalm 14 Elohim appears three times and Jehovah four times, while in Psalm 53 the word is Elohim in every instance. If Psalm 14 is the original psalm, as most commentators think, it is hard to explain the change of Jehovah to Elohim in Psalm 53, except to say that Jehovah is the word for God that predominates in book 1 of the Psalter while Elohim predominates in book 2.

The only significant variation in Psalm 53 is verse 5, which replaces verses 5 and 6 of Psalm 14. The earlier psalm seems to be addressing fools in Israel, because it refers to them as being "in the company of the righteous." It says:

❧ **Psalm 53** ❧

There they are, overwhelmed with dread,
    for God is present in the company of the righteous.
You evildoers frustrate the plans of the poor,
    but the LORD is their refuge.

The later psalm is addressing evildoers who have attacked Israel, presumably Gentiles, whom it refers to saying:

There they were, overwhelmed with dread,
    where there was nothing to dread.
God scattered the bones of those who attacked you;
    you put them to shame, for God despised them.

We can only guess what specific incident this refers to, but something like the scattering of the armies of Sennacherib in the days of Hezekiah and Isaiah would explain it well (cf. 2 Kings 18–19). If verse 5 does refer to the defeat of alien armies in the time of one of these kings, then a later poet probably altered David's original psalm to apply it more intently and specifically to the new situation.

On the other hand, if David wrote this psalm as it stands and if it was written during the period of his life when he was escaping from King Saul, then the psalm might be David's observations on the nature and final end of those who were making life difficult for him. Since Psalm 53 follows Psalm 52, which deals with Doeg, it may be a commentary on the nature of that very ruthless man. We remember that Doeg was an Edomite, not a Jew, even though he was in the close employ of King Saul. David had many enemies, however, and it may also be the case that the psalm is a general description of the folly of those who act as if there is no God. It is a valuable word about those who act as if there is no God today.

∽ Psalm 53 ∽

Fools and Their Folly

We are looking at these psalms for what they tell us about David and the way he approached bad times. One clue to how we might deal with the psalm, particularly verses 1–3, is to look at it as Paul did when he quoted the opening verses in Romans. He used it as part of his analysis of the way the human race has rejected God. In that analysis the fool of the psalm is one who knows about God's existence because of God's revelation of himself in nature but who suppresses that knowledge because he does not want to acknowledge God. That is sin, of course. So recognizing that it is sin, we could define a fool by saying, "A fool is anyone who sins by acting as if there is no God."

David must have known many people like this, and Doeg would have been one of them. If we approach Psalm 53 in this way, we can look at it for what David has to teach about sin, its nature, its fruit, and its consequences. Matthew Henry did that. He found eight points in the psalm, seven of which have to do with sin and the eighth, by contrast, with the faith of the saints. All begin with the letter *f*. I am adopting his outline for what follows.[2]

1. *The fact of sin.* Henry begins with the reality of sin, arguing his point from the fact that "God looks down from heaven" and sees it (v. 2). You and I do not always see sin, and the chief reason for our blindness is that we choose to close our eyes to transgressions. We often do that with others, turning a blind eye to their actions. We nearly always do it with ourselves. If we are confronted with the reality of our sin, we defend ourselves with such excuses as "I didn't mean to do it," "You don't understand what happened," "It wasn't really like that," "It wasn't my fault," or "You should have seen what the other

person did to me first." In other words, we pretend either that the act was not sin or that it was justified.

In the Garden of Eden, on the occasion of the first sin, Adam tried to deny his fault by blaming Eve: "The woman you put here with me—she gave me some fruit from the tree, and I ate it" (Gen. 3:12).

Eve blamed Satan: "The serpent deceived me, and I ate" (v. 13).

The problem with denial is that we are not the court of last appeal. In fact, we are not even judges. We are the accused, and the one who knows the facts of the case, prepares the indictment, handles the prosecution, and renders the ultimate judgment is God. The omniscient God sees perfectly and knows all things. Before him all hearts are open, all desires known, and it is he who says:

> Everyone has turned away,
>   they have together become corrupt;
> there is no one who does good,
>   not even one.
>
> Psalm 53:3

It will do us no good to pretend that sin is not sin or that we are not sinners, as long as God is on his throne.

2. *The fault of sin.* Another way we deal with sin so we can live with it and not feel too guilty is to minimize sin, thinking of sin as a weakness or imperfection perhaps but certainly not as a serious transgression that inevitably harms us and wounds others. It is evidence of our folly that we do this, but God is no fool and he tells it like it is.

God says that sinners are "corrupt" and that "their ways are vile" (v. 1). He describes them as having "turned away" from the correct path (v. 3). He says that they are "evildoers" who "devour" other people (v. 4). These terms describe sin accurately in terms of three basic relationships—our relationships to God, ourselves, and others. As far as God is concerned, we have turned from him. Indeed, the verb is even stronger than this: It means that we have turned around entirely and are now pursuing a completely "anti-God" path. We have become corrupt and vile. We are destroying ourselves, and our sin is offensive both to God and others. We are also harming others by our actions. Sin is no small thing. It is very harmful.

3. *The fountain of sin.* "How comes it that men are so bad?" asks Henry. "Surely it is because there is no fear of God before their eyes."[3] It is because they say in their hearts, "There is no God" (v. 1).

This does not necessarily describe what we would call theoretical atheism—that is, the atheism of one who literally denies the existence of a Supreme Being. We have quite a few theoretical atheists in our day, but an atheist like this was rare in the ancient world. What is in view here is rather what we might call practical atheism, the outlook of one who would concede that there is a God but who would maintain that God has nothing to do with the world as it now is and therefore God has no practical bearing on how we are to live or what we do. This is clearer in the Hebrew text than in the English translation, because in Hebrew the words *there is* in the phrase "there is no God" are missing, and the text actually says, "No God"— that is, "No God for me." Regardless of whether he thinks God exists, the fool does not act as if God is there.

This is the source of our troubles, of course. Psalm 8 says that God has placed man in a mediating position in the universe, midway between God and the angelic beings, who are above him, and the animals or beasts, who are below. It is man's privilege and duty to look up and so become increasingly like the one to whom he looks. But if man will not look up, if he determines to act as if "there is no God," then the only way he can look is down, in the direction of the animals, and as a result he will begin to behave like them. In fact, he will behave even worse than animals. He will multiply sin and invent new ways of doing evil (Rom. 1:30). His path will be downhill, and there will be no depths to which he will not go.

I have noticed by reading the newspapers and news-magazines that as soon as people get disturbed by this obvi-ously downward inclination and begin to search for standards, "community standards" beyond which we will not go, that is precisely where the culture does go. Sinners embrace the vice as soon as it is mentioned, so great is our self-destroying, beast-like, lemminglike run into the sea.

4. *The folly of sin.* This is utter folly, of course, the fourth of Henry's points. It is folly because God exists, whether we acknowledge him or not, and because it is certain that one day we will have to stand before him to give an accounting of every word we have spoken and every deed we have done. If you are a person who has been living as if there is no God, what do you suppose you will say to God on that day? What excuse will you make?

"I didn't know you existed"?

How do you think that will sound to God, who has gone to such lengths to reveal himself to you? He has revealed him-self in creation, in Jesus Christ, and in the Bible. Have you taken time to study creation for its revelation of God? To inves-tigate the "claims of Jesus Christ"? To read the Bible?

"I didn't think you were important"?

How insulting to God! You thought television was impor-tant, the latest football or baseball scores were important, your bank account was important. Didn't you think God was impor-tant? Can you imagine how offensive that will sound to the exalted, almighty, all-wise God?

∽ **Psalm 53** ∾

"I didn't have time for you"?

You had time for everything else, everything you believed was important. If you have not exerted yourself to know God and to love and serve him with all your heart, mind, soul, and strength, you will be revealed as the greatest of all fools on the day you must give an accounting. And you will know that you were a fool, whether you will acknowledge it openly or not.

5. *The filthiness of sin.* One of the deceptive features of sin is that it masquerades as something beautiful and desirable while actually it is hideous and destructive. The words the psalm uses are *corrupt* and *vile* (v. 1).

When Magic Johnson, the handsome professional basketball player, revealed that he had AIDS (Acquired Immune Deficiency Syndrome), the first reaction of the sportswriters and pundits was jubilation that at last we had an attractive way to look at the killer disease. One newspaper I read actually spoke of the "smiling face of AIDS," because Magic Johnson is so often seen smiling. Another paper said that we now know that AIDS is not a danger only for some groups of people but that anyone can get it. That is not true, of course. AIDS is not acquired by those who obey the moral law of God, except in a few tragic cases involving the transfusion of contaminated blood. As far as the "smiling face of AIDS" is concerned—well, anyone can smile at the beginning. It is the end that is horrible, and there are few deaths that are as horrible as those of AIDS sufferers.

The Bible says, "There is a way that seems right to a man, but in the end it leads to death" (Prov. 14:12). Paul wrote, "The wages of sin is death, but the gift of God is eternal life in Christ Jesus our Lord" (Rom. 6:23).

6. *The fruit of sin.* Sin destroys the one who pursues it, of course. But Psalm 53:4 also shows how it impacts others. The verse uses a simple image, describing evildoers as "those who

devour my people as men eat bread." In the Middle East, as
in the Western world, bread is the most common of food sta-
ples. It is eaten regularly and with scarcely a thought. This
seems to be how the psalmist regards evildoers as acting when
they further their own interests. They devour the weak and
poor in order that they might grow strong and rich themselves.
What an apt description of our own "dog-eat-dog" world! We
know people who function exactly like that. They don't care
what happens to anyone else. Underneath the glamour, that
is sin's true nature.

The righteous do care what happens to others. Therefore,
they will do the right thing even at great personal cost, and
they are generous with what is theirs in order to help others.

7. *The fear and shame that attends sin.* Verse 5 is the verse that
is the new addition and variant in this repeated psalm, and it
seems to refer to a historical incident, though we cannot be
sure which one. I have already mentioned the scattering of the
armies of Sennacherib in the days of Hezekiah as a possibility (2 Kings 18–19), but there are numerous examples of God
sending unreasoning terror into the hearts of Israel's foes.
Joshua 10:10 tells of the confusion of the armies of southern
Canaan when the Jewish troops fell on them at Gibeon. Judges
7 recounts the battle of Gideon and his small army of three
hundred men against the Midianites, when all they did was
surround the Midianite camp by night, expose their lanterns,
and blow their trumpets. The Midianites were terrified and
turned against one another, killing their own countrymen in
the night. In 1 Samuel 14, after Jonathan and his armor bearer
had killed some twenty of the Philistines, "panic struck the
whole army" and Saul and his army routed them (v. 15).

In these cases, panic overtook Israel's enemies when there
was no adequate human cause for it. But if that has been so
when there was no cause, how much greater the fear will be

when sinners are confronted by the enormity of their transgression before the presence of the thrice holy God. Jesus said of sinners that in the day of God's judgment, "They will say to the mountains, 'Fall on us!' and to the hills, 'Cover us!'" so great will be their dread (Luke 23:30). But the hills will answer to God who created them, not those who have been opposed to him, and the wicked will be forced to give an accounting of all they have done.

The Faith of the Saints

The last of Matthew Henry's points maintains the alliteration of words beginning with the letter *f* (the fact, fault, fountain, folly, filthiness, fruit, and fear of sin). But the last point turns from sin to the contrasting portrait of the true people of God found in verse 6. Henry calls this verse "The faith of the saints."

These people live in a world in which fools do indeed act and speak as if "there is no God." It is a world in which sin abounds and in which the perpetrators of evil habitually destroy the righteous as those who eat bread. But in the midst of this present evil world, made cruel by sin, the saints look upward and wait for the salvation that comes from Zion. In the days of the psalmist that salvation was still in the future, for properly assessed it was not an earthly deliverance from such threats as the Canaanite, Midianite, Philistine, or Assyrian armies. These were temporary, physical deliverances. The "salvation" to which the righteous looked was God himself, particularly the Messiah whose coming had been foretold many times in the Old Testament.

That Messiah was Jesus. So now, we who live on the after side of his coming look back to him as the one who alone delivers us from sin. We put our faith in him and his work, rather than in our own works, as the basis of our salvation. And we look forward to his second coming too, knowing that in that day sin will be punished, good will be rewarded, and the folly of those who have lived as if there is no God will be revealed. You can be encouraged by that if you are surrounded by godless people who have taken advantage of you without any thought of their ultimate accountability.

If you have been living as if there is no God, I urge you to repent of your folly and become wise instead. The person who is wise knows that he or she needs a Savior. When that Savior is revealed, the wise person believes on him and follows him forever.

Psalm 54

Save me, O God, by your name;
   vindicate me by your might.
Hear my prayer, O God;
   listen to the words of my mouth.

Strangers are attacking me;
   ruthless men seek my life—
   men without regard for God.   *Selah*

Surely God is my help;
   the Lord is the one who sustains me.

Let evil recoil on those who slander me;
   in your faithfulness destroy them.

I will sacrifice a freewill offering to you;
   I will praise your name, O LORD,
     for it is good.
For he has delivered me from all my troubles,
   and my eyes have looked in triumph on my foes.

Betrayed

It is not always possible to trace a connection between psalms, but sometimes it is, and that is the case with Psalm 54 and those that surround it. Psalm 54 follows nicely after Psalm 53. The earlier psalm was about people who act as if "there is no God," the moral and spiritual "fools" of this world. In Psalm 54 the psalmist is surrounded by just such people. He speaks of them as "ruthless men . . . men without regard for God" (v. 3). The earlier psalm ends with the faith of the saints—that is, the faith of believers living in just such a world.

Psalm 54 is also about betrayal, and that links it not only to Psalm 52, which describes David's betrayal by Doeg the Edomite, but also to Psalm 55, which speaks of David's betrayal by a close friend. What is most important perhaps is that betrayal links David's experience to our own, because there is probably not one of us who has not felt betrayed at some time by someone close to us—a husband or wife, child, parent, employer, someone we have helped at our own cost, or someone we once trusted with our inmost feelings or the most personal details of our lives. What we need to learn from this psalm is how David dealt with his disappointment.

Psalm 52 and Psalm 54 are also intertwined historically since, according to their titles, they came from the same period in David's life, the time when he was fleeing from King Saul.

You will recall from study of the earlier psalm that David had fled suddenly on advice from his close friend Jonathan, Saul's son. He had gone to the priestly city of Nob and had been given food and the sword of Goliath, which had been stored there since the day he had killed the great Philistine champion. The evil man Doeg was present when David arrived, and sometime later Doeg revealed that David had gone to Nob and had been helped by Ahimelech, the chief priest of Nob. You will remember that Saul turned on Ahimelech, demanding his death, and when the soldiers refused to lift their hands against God's priest, Doeg obliged the king by killing not only Ahimelech but his entire family and all the other priests and families of Nob. Eighty-five priests were killed, and the inhabitants of Nob were massacred. Only one man, Abiathar, a son of Ahimelech, escaped to tell David what happened.

David felt responsible. It was one of the darkest moments of David's life.

The immediate background for Psalm 54 picks up at this point. According to 1 Samuel 23, the Philistines were attacking a Jewish border town called Keilah. David asked God whether he should attack the Philistines and rescue the citizens of Keilah, and when God gave him leave to do so, he drove the Philistines off and rescued the endangered city. Keilah was a walled city. So when news came to Saul, who was still pursuing David, that David was in Keilah, Saul marched his armies south to capture him. He said, "David has imprisoned himself by entering a town with gates and bars" (v. 7).

Abiathar, the son of Ahimelech who had escaped to David after the massacre of the priests of Nob, had brought with him the sacred ephod, used to discern the will of God in specific situations. David used it to ask whether the citizens of Keilah, whom he had just rescued, would deliver him over to Saul if

Saul surrounded the city, and he was told that they would indeed surrender him to Saul. So David slipped out of the city before Saul arrived and went south into the hills of the desert area of Ziph.

Even in this remote area David was not safe. When he was in Horesh, one of the towns of this region, the Ziphites went to Saul at Gibeah to tell him where David was hiding. They said, "Is not David hiding among us in the strongholds at Horesh, on the hill of Hakilah, south of Jeshimon? [It was a very specific set of directions.] Now, O king, come down whenever it pleases you to do so, and we will be responsible for handing him over to the king" (1 Sam. 23:19–20). It pleased Saul to do so right away. So he moved against David, pursuing him out of Horesh into the southern wilderness before he was forced to break off to defend the country against the Philistines who were invading further north.

Even this was not the end of David's trouble or the Ziphites' treachery. Later, when David and his men were hiding in Hakilah in the same southern region, the Ziphites went to Saul again and reported, "Is not David hiding on the hill of Hakilah, which faces Jeshimon?" (1 Sam. 26:1). The title of Psalm 54 refers to these betrayals by the people of Ziph when it says, "When the Ziphites had gone to Saul and said, 'Is not David hiding among us?'"

So this was a bad period for David, a time when it seemed he had nowhere to turn. He was unsafe even in the wilderness, and there was hardly anyone he could trust. He had saved one of the cities of his tribesmen in the south, but even these people were against him. Derek Kidner says, "To be betrayed by Doeg the Edomite had been hardly a surprise (1 Sam. 22:22), but now David finds himself rejected by men of his own tribe."[1] He was rejected, pursued, betrayed. But it was out of this dark, dangerous, and disillusioning situation that he called upon God in the words of Psalm 54 and found God to be his sure and steadfast help.

This is a psalm for anyone who feels abandoned, rejected, or betrayed. Do you feel that no one is on your side, that no one cares for you? You need to do what David did and turn to God. In this psalm we see what that means and how David did it.

The Fugitive's God

One lesson we learn from David is that whenever he had a problem he brought it to God. This is what he does in the opening part of this psalm (vv. 1–3). In other words, he prayed. If Joseph Scriven's popular hymn of 1855, "What a Friend We Have in Jesus," had been known in David's day, he would have understood it and identified with it completely:

> Have we trials and temptations?
> Is there trouble anywhere?
> We should never be discouraged
> Take it to the Lord in prayer.

> Can we find a Friend so faithful
> Who will all our sorrows share?
> Jesus knows our every weakness—
> Take it to the Lord in prayer.

> Do thy friends despise, forsake thee?
> Take it to the Lord in prayer;
> In His arms He'll take and shield thee,
> Thou wilt find a solace there.

So David prayed. But equally important is the fact that he prayed to God; that is, he prayed to the true God whom he had come to know by studying Scripture and by personal experience. He reminds us how important this is by saying in the first line of the psalm, "Save me, O God, by your name" (v. 1).

What does David mean when he asks God to save him "by your name"? That idea does not have a great deal of importance for us, because we do not often think of a name itself being particularly significant. We think of God but not the name of God. For the Old Testament saints it was different. For them names were important generally. They were understood to sum up the character and personality of the person named. That is why there are so many descriptive or symbolic names in the Old Testament and why we find such significant episodes as God naming one of the Old Testament characters or one of these characters inquiring after the name of God. We remember how Jacob inquired after the name of God when he wrestled with him at the brook Jabbok (Gen. 32:29) and was given a new name himself.

Moses asked God for his name when God called him at the burning bush:

> "Suppose I go to the Israelites and say to them, 'The God of your fathers has sent me to you,' and they ask me, 'What is his name?' Then what shall I tell them?"
>
> God said to Moses, "I AM WHO I AM. This is what you are to say to the Israelites: 'I AM has sent me to you.'"
>
> Exodus 3:13–14

This example is particularly important for understanding Psalm 54. For the name God gave Moses, "I AM" (Yahweh or Jehovah, usually translated "LORD"), is the name David is appealing to in this psalm.

Notice how he does it, heightening the importance of the name by delaying pronouncing it until verse 6. The psalm begins, "Save me, O God, by your name." But the word for God in the opening verse is not Jehovah but Elohim, the name most often used for God in the second book of the Psalter. Moreover, this is the name that prevails up to and including verse 4. It is in verse 2, "Hear my prayer, O *God*." We have it again in verse 3, "men without regard for *God*," and again in verse 4, "Surely *God* is my help."

Verse 4 goes a step further by introducing the title Adonai (usually translated "Lord"). But it is not until verse 6 that the name appealed to in the opening sentence is actually introduced. Verse 6 reads literally: "I will sacrifice a freewill offering to you; I will praise your name, O *Jehovah (Yahweh)*, for it is good."

Scholars are divided on the exact meaning of the name Jehovah, but that is only because it is so great and so encompassing that nothing we can say ever seems to do it justice. The name is the root of the Hebrew verb *to be,* which is why it is translated "I AM" in Exodus 3:14. It is in the present tense, of course, revealing God as the eternal present—that is, as the one who has always existed and who will always exist, the unchangeable God. Eternal existence also implies self-existence and self-sufficiency. Self-existence means that God has no origins and is therefore answerable to no one. He does not owe us explanations for his actions. Self-sufficiency means that God depends on no one and therefore has no needs. God helps those who call on him, but he needs no help himself. He does not need helpers; he does not need defenders; he does not even need worshipers. But he is what we need. We often find ourselves in situations that have no conceivable human solution. Our circumstances may be impossible, but they are not impossible for God. Jesus said, "With God all things are possible" (Matt. 19:26).

❧ **Psalm 54** ☙

The Fugitive's Prayer

After the opening cry of verse 1, which sets the theme for the psalm, David prays, asking Jehovah to rescue him in his forsaken situation. His prayer has the following five parts.

1. *He asks God to hear his lament (v. 2).* When Jesus prayed, he said on one occasion, "Father, I [know] that you always hear me" (John 11:42). It is also true that God always hears us in the sense that he knows all things and therefore obviously also hears all things. Nevertheless, it is good for us to ask God to hear us. For the very act of asking reminds us of who God is and that there are things that, if they do not hinder him from hearing us, at least hinder him from responding when we ask. Sin is one such hindrance. That is why God said through Isaiah:

> Surely the arm of the LORD is not too short to save,
>   nor his ear too dull to hear.
> But your iniquities have separated
>   you from your God;
> your sins have hidden his face from you,
>   so that he will not hear.
>
> Isaiah 59:1–2

When we ask God to hear us, as David's example encourages us to do, we should take time to see if there is any reason why God should not hear us. If there is a reason, we must confess the sin or correct the situation.

2. *He describes the situation he faces (v. 3).* Some people are reluctant to say if something is bothering them or admit they have a problem, probably because they want to save face or keep up appearances. Christians are often among their number, even when they are talking to God. But not David. One of the most refreshing aspects of the psalms written by David

is that he is not the least hesitant to say what he thinks or describe a situation as he sees it. In this verse he says that he is being attacked by ruthless men. These men have no regard for God, and what they want to do is kill him. That was literally true, of course. Saul was seeking his life. Those who were loyal to Saul were part of Saul's evil design, and David never knew when someone who seemed to be his friend might betray his whereabouts in hopes of securing the present king's favor.

If you are facing some hard problem, I encourage you to tell God about it in detail. God knows it already, of course. But it will do you good to spell it out, and mentioning details will remind you that God also knows them and cares about them. You will also be reminding yourself that he cares for you.

3. *He encourages himself by remembering who God is (v. 4)*. David does not merely wallow in his problems. There is a danger of doing that when we lay our troubles before God, but David does not fall into that trap. As soon as he has described his situation (v. 3), he breaks off completely and spends the rest of his time reminding himself of who God truly is. "Surely God is my help; the Lord is the one who sustains me."

In 1 Peter 5:7 the apostle who had learned to trust Jesus rather than himself in all situations says, "Cast all your anxiety on him because he cares for you." (The very next psalm is where Peter got that text; cf. Ps. 55:22.) In Psalm 54 David has cast his anxiety on God. That is what verses 1 through 3 have been about. Now, having done it, he is ready to encourage himself by remembering that God is indeed his help and that God has been sustaining him and will continue to sustain him in his difficulties. It is what Isaac Watts captured so well in his poetic rendering of Psalm 90:

> Our God, our Help in ages past,
> Our Hope for years to come,

ᗡ Psalm 54 ᗡ

> Be thou our Guard while troubles last
> And our eternal Home!

4. *He makes his request (v. 5).* Finally, David makes the specific request that God would destroy those who were attacking him. In the case of Doeg, pictured in Psalm 52, he has already prophesied what his end would be. He was to be pulled down, snatched up, twisted out, and torn from Israel, even from the land of the living (Ps. 52:5). David is not so graphic in Psalm 54, but he does pray that evil might "recoil on those who slander" him and that God might be faithful by destroying them.

This prayer has bothered a number of commentators, who say that this is somehow unworthy of a man of God and that we have been taught better in the New Testament. For example, A. Weiser complains about "human self-will and man's low instincts of vindictiveness and gloating," suggesting that the proper response is to pray for one's enemies.[2] It is true, of course, that we have been taught to pray for our enemies. But that does not mean that we are to cease to care for righteousness or pray that justice should be done by God. It is worth noting that judgment did eventually come to David's enemies. David was right to pray for it.

It is equally important, however, to remember that when David had the opportunity, he did not take justice against Saul into his own hands. The chapters that provide the background for Psalms 52 and 54 tell how David received what seemed to be "God-given" opportunities to kill Saul and record how he spared Saul's life on at least two occasions (cf. 1 Sam. 24, 26).

5. *He promises God a freewill offering (vv. 6–7).* This is not a case of offering a bribe to God, saying "I will bring you an offering if you deliver me from my enemies." This is a thank offering, promised to God in advance of his deliverance on

the grounds of his firm confidence that God would indeed deliver him. How does he know God will do it? It is because of who God is ("God is my help"), and because God has delivered him in the past. David may not have begun this psalm with confidence. But having brought his anxieties to God and having reminded himself of who God is, he finds, as he did in so many other psalms, that he is restored to a quiet trust and confidence in God by the end of it.

Charles Haddon Spurgeon wrote, "Let us trust that if we are as friendless as this man of God, we may resort to prayer as he did, exercise the like faith, and find ourselves ere long singing the same joyous hymn of praise."[3]

Man of Sorrows

Here is one last thought. When we are studying the psalms we must be careful not to turn them all into prophecies of the coming of Jesus Christ or of events of his or the very last days. Saint Augustine did. He interpreted almost everything in them as a prophecy of Christ. Likewise, Arno Gaebelein saw nearly everything as a prophecy of the experience of Israel just before the Lord's second coming. These narrow perspectives greatly limit the value of their commentaries. Most of the psalms are not prophecy at all, but a few are. These are the Messianic psalms. And there are other psalms that, although they are not about Jesus Christ specifically, nevertheless aptly describe what we know were his experiences from the account we have of them in the New Testament.

Psalm 54 may be in this latter category. If we study it with the passion of Christ in mind, we find it an excellent expression of the hope of the one who called on God in his suffering and was heard by him.

⋘ **Psalm 54** ⋙

> Save me, O God, by your name.
> Strangers are attacking me.
> Surely God is my help.
> He has delivered me from all my troubles.

The Father did hear, did help, and did save Jesus, even as he heard, helped, and saved David. Remember that Jesus understands what is happening to you. If you call to him, you can be sure that he will also hear you and help you.

Psalm 55

Listen to my prayer, O God,
 do not ignore my plea;
  hear me and answer me.
My thoughts trouble me and I am distraught
 at the voice of the enemy,
  at the stares of the wicked;
for they bring down suffering upon me
 and revile me in their anger.

My heart is in anguish within me;
 the terrors of death assail me.
Fear and trembling have beset me;
 horror has overwhelmed me.
I said, "Oh, that I had the wings of a dove!
 I would fly away and be at rest—
I would flee far away
 and stay in the desert;   *Selah*
I would hurry to my place of shelter,
 far from the tempest and storm."

Confuse the wicked, O Lord, confound their speech,
 for I see violence and strife in the city.
Day and night they prowl about on its walls;
 malice and abuse are within it.
Destructive forces are at work in the city;
 threats and lies never leave its streets.

If an enemy were insulting me,
    I could endure it;
if a foe were raising himself against me,
    I could hide from him.
But it is you, a man like myself,
    my companion, my close friend,
with whom I once enjoyed sweet fellowship
    as we walked with the throng at the house of God.

Let death take my enemies by surprise;
    let them go down alive to the grave,
    for evil finds lodging among them.

But I call to God,
    and the LORD saves me.
Evening, morning and noon
    I cry out in distress,
    and he hears my voice.
He ransoms me unharmed
    from the battle waged against me,
    even though many oppose me.
God, who is enthroned forever,
    will hear them and afflict them—   *Selah*
men who never change their ways
    and have no fear of God.

My companion attacks his friends;
    he violates his covenant.
His speech is smooth as butter,
    yet war is in his heart;
his words are more soothing than oil,
    yet they are drawn swords. . . .

Betrayed by a Close Friend

As I pointed out in the last chapter, the psalms sometimes have meaningful relationships to one another, and that is the case with Psalms 52, 54, and 55. According to their titles, each is by David and each involves David's betrayal by some person or group of people. In Psalm 52 David was betrayed by a foreigner—Doeg the Edomite. In Psalm 54 David was betrayed by the people of Ziph—that is, by his own countrymen. This short series of betrayal psalms reaches a strong climax in Psalm 55 with its description of David's betrayal by an intimate friend.

Who was this friend? The best guess is Ahithophel, David's most trusted counselor, who sided with Absalom at the time of Absalom's rebellion. But this is a "best guess" only because we have no other story from David's life to link it to. Ahithophel's story is told in 2 Samuel 15–17. It tells us that he was close to David and that he betrayed him in order to side with Absalom, later hanging himself when Absalom rejected his advice in favor of another counselor.

Yet there are problems with this view. The writer of Psalm 55 is presumably in Jerusalem. But in the account of Absalom's rebellion given in 2 Samuel, David learned of Ahithophel's defection only after he had left that city. Again, although David valued the advice of Ahithophel and trusted him, it would be hard to say that he was as close to David as Psalm 55 describes the betrayer having been: "my companion, my close friend, with whom I once enjoyed sweet fellowship" (vv. 13–14).

These difficulties have caused some commentators to ascribe the psalm to another writer entirely, to Jeremiah or to someone writing in a later, declining period of the monarchy. But the title says the psalm is by David, and we should probably assume that it is merely about an incident that is not recounted in the historical books. At best those books give a summary of what was obviously a long and very complex career.

What about an outline for the psalm? Many commentators offer a three-part outline. For example, G. Campbell Morgan divides it like this: (1) fear (vv. 1–8), (2) fury (vv. 9–15), and (3) faith (vv. 16–23).[1] Marvin E. Tate, one of the more modern commentators, divides it into ten parts.[2]

In my judgment, the best way of getting into the psalm is to focus on its alternating pattern of six or seven parts. This has occurred in the Psalter before, in Psalms 5, 18, 42, and 43, for example. In the case of Psalm 55, the stanzas alternate between disclosures of the psalmist's state of mind and his descriptions of the wicked who are causing him problems. As is usual with such psalms, the descriptions of the psalmist's state show improvement as David moves from great anguish and pain to quiet confidence in God.

I outline the psalm like this: (1) the first disclosure of the psalmist's anguish (vv. 1–8), (2) the first description of the wicked (vv. 9–11), (3) the second disclosure of the psalmist's anguish (vv. 12–14), (4) the second description of the wicked (v. 15), (5) the psalmist's faith in God

(vv. 16–19), (6) the third description of the wicked (vv. 20–21), and (7) the psalmist's final conclusion and advice (vv. 22–23).[3] The psalm is part lament, part prayer, and part wisdom literature.

The Psalmist's Personal Anguish

There is a significant difference between the setting of the two earlier psalms of betrayal and this one. In Psalms 52 and 54 David is in the wilderness fleeing from his enemy Saul, a low point in his career, while in Psalm 55 he is apparently established in Jerusalem, his capital city. This must mean that Saul is dead and that David is now king. We would expect this situation to be good. David's troubles should be over. But we find that this is not the case and that David is as much troubled in his ascendancy as he was when a fugitive.

In fact, the pain of these verses (vv. 1–8) may even be greater, for this is strong language. David begins by saying that he is "distraught" (v. 2) and in "anguish" (v. 4), and the words increase in intensity after this. The "terrors of death" assail him (v. 4). "Fear and trembling" beset him (v. 5). "Horror" overwhelms him (v. 5).

In verses 6 through 8 we find something new. The writer is so distraught by what he finds around him that he is thinking about how wonderful it would be to escape from his troubles. We have not seen anything like this before in David's psalms. He has been fearful before. He has anguished over evil. But always he has seemed ready in God's power to confront the evil boldly. Nowhere before has he expressed a wish to escape his trouble, to fly away and be at rest.

> I said, "Oh, that I had the wings of a dove!
> I would fly away and be at rest—

Psalm 55

> I would flee far away
>   and stay in the desert;
>   I would hurry to my place of shelter,
>   far from the tempest and storm."
>
> verses 6–8

What is happening? Why do we find this new element? In my opinion, what we have here is the weariness that comes to a valiant warrior or worker late in life or at least after the passing of youthful battles and triumphs. When we are young we do not expect life to be easy, and if we are energetic, we tackle problems with optimism and with our full strength. We achieve certain victories too. But as life goes on we find that the problems we thought we had overcome earlier are still around. The company we work for is still in trouble. Our taxes are still high. The murder and felony rates have not declined. Our children continue to cause trouble. In addition, we are getting older and therefore have less energy to cope with problems. We find ourselves thinking how nice it would be merely to fly away and escape them.

Many do, of course, at least if they have sufficient money to retire and travel. That desire makes the tourist industry flourish. But it is not always possible to escape things—David did not have "the wings of a dove"—and God does not always allow us to leave either, especially if the problems we face involve continuing responsibilities or commitments.

At this point the psalm becomes a lesson to us in steady perseverance, particularly perseverance in middle or late age. Perseverance is one of the virtues God looks for in his children, which is why the apostle Paul wrote, "We also rejoice in our sufferings, because we know that suffering produces perseverance; perseverance, character; and character, hope" (Rom. 5:3–4).

∞ Psalm 55 ∞

Bad Times in the City

Having unburdened himself of his troubled inner feelings, the psalmist now turns to the wicked who are wreaking havoc in the city. His description of this evil is in words people who live in cities in our day can readily understand (vv. 9–11).

We might have thought from David's reference to "the enemy" in verse 3 that he was concerned about the hostile nations that surrounded the Jewish kingdom. But now we discover that the enemy is not without but within. The psalmist is saying, as Pogo said in one of the best-known Pogo cartoons, "We have met the enemy, and he is us." These verses personify six vices in three pairs of two each. Violence and Strife prowl about on its walls. Malice and Abuse are within the city. Threats and Lies never leave the streets. It is a grim picture, because we know that these are not just forces in themselves. They are present because wicked people are present, and these wicked people are within the gates. They are us.

That is what is wrong with the cities of America, of course. We want to blame our problems on the environment or government programs or the lack of government programs. But the problem is not "out there." It is within. The problem is that we are sinners, and this means that there will never be a substantial improvement in the moral state of our cities (or the country as a whole for that matter) until there is a deep moral improvement in America's people. And that happens in only one way, by revival of a people rediscovering God. There is nothing America needs so much at the present time as a Holy Spirit–produced revival and reformation.

But until that comes we can at least pray that evil will be frustrated and the doers of evil confused. This is what David prays for in verse 9, asking God to "confuse the wicked" and "confound their speech," using words deliberately reminiscent of the confusion God brought upon the builders of the tower of Babel (cf. Gen. 11:1–9). God does it too. Thank God he does. We would be many times worse off if evil people could actually get their acts together and work in harmony against the righteous instead of fighting among themselves, as they habitually do.

The Psalmist's Pain

It is possible to see verses 12 through 14 as an extension of the psalmist's description of the evil in Jerusalem, but it is better to view them as a return to the revelation of his own anguish and pain. In fact, like a trained psychologist probing deeply for the root of his pain, David explores his own heart and reveals that what is bothering him most is that his own close friend has betrayed him. The friend's betrayal is part of the general evil, of course. If this is a reference to the days of Absalom's rebellion, it might even have greatly contributed to it. But more than this, the betrayal is the root of David's personal pain and his understandable desire to run away from what is hurting him and be at rest.

How well he knows himself and how well he describes the situation:

> If an enemy were insulting me,
>   I could endure it;
> if a foe were raising himself against me,
>   I could hide from him.
>
> verse 12

He had endured attacks from enemies, of course, and hid. When David was fleeing Jerusalem and Shimei, a noted enemy, cursed him from the hillside, crying, "Get out, get out, you man of blood, you scoundrel! The LORD has repaid you for all the blood you shed in the household of Saul, in whose place you have reigned," the king did not allow his men to retaliate by killing Shimei. He said, "My son, who is of my own flesh, is trying to take my life. How much more then, this Benjamite! . . . It may be that the LORD will see my distress and repay me with good for the cursing I am receiving today" (2 Sam. 16:5–14).

David bore Shimei's cursing well. But this was not Shimei, an enemy. This was his companion, his close friend, one with whom he had enjoyed sweet fellowship, a person in whose presence he had worshiped at the house of God. It is no revelation to say that it is those who are closest to us who hurt us most. Spurgeon said, "None are such real enemies as false friends."[4]

Destruction for the Wicked

Verse 15 seems to stand alone. It is the low point of the psalm and is a prayer or wish in which David longs for the destruction of his foes. The language is important because, just as verse 9 uses words that deliberately recall the confusion of speech at the building of the tower of Babel, so here the throwback is to the destruction of Korah and his followers in the days of Moses. On that occasion "the ground under them split apart and the earth opened its mouth and swallowed them, with their households and all Korah's men and all their possessions. They went down alive into the grave, with everything they owned; the earth closed over them, and they perished and were gone from the community" (Num. 16:31–33). David is referring to this unprecedented destruction in the words of verse 15.

But why the vehemence? J. J. Stewart Perowne explains it by his friend's betrayal: "To have trusted, and to find his trust betrayed; to have been one with a man in public and in private, bound to him by personal ties, and by the ties of religion, and then to find honor, faith, affection, all cast to the winds—this it was that seemed so terrible, this it was that called for the withering curse."[5]

That may be, of course. But it seems significant that David does not specifically mention his former friend in this malediction. In fact, he seems to have distinguished between his enemies, who are cursed here, and his former friend in the previous section, who is not cursed.

A Turning Point in the Psalm

What is important is that a turning point comes with verse 16. Earlier the writer had called on God. The psalm began, "Listen to my prayer, O God, do not ignore my plea; hear me and answer me" (vv. 1–2). But that was uttered out of the writer's anguish. Here the tone is different. In these words the psalmist explains that when he calls on God, as he has just done, the Lord actually hears him and saves him. He explains his experiences of God's grace in three moving phrases: "The LORD saves me" (v. 16), "He hears my voice" (v. 17), and "He ransoms me unharmed" (v. 18). Because of this past experience of God's grace, which the psalmist has remembered, he knows that God will destroy the enemies that still confront him and will deliver him from them (v. 19). This is faith, of course. It is the point we come to when problems are honestly faced and brought to God.

Brought to God again and again, I should add. For that is the point of the alternating structure of the psalm. There are psalms that are short, fierce statements of concern, thrown up to God in quick desperation. But this is not one of them. This is a prayer in which the psalmist unburdens himself of his anguish, describes the terrors he is facing, reflects on the evil of his foes, asks God for help, and then lays the same things before God again. In other words, this is a lesson in perseverance.

It is also an illustration of how such persevering prayer first changes us, strengthening our faith, before God intervenes in response to change our desperate situation.

A Final Glance at the Wicked

The alternating structure of the psalm continues in verses 20 and 21 where David casts a final glance at the friend who has betrayed him. But the tone has changed again. Earlier David was deeply pained by the betrayal. Here, having laid the matter before God and having assured himself that God is his Savior and that he will surely deliver him from such evil, David steps away from his own feelings and reflects on the wrongdoing itself. The real problem is that the man is a covenant breaker, and the reason he breaks covenants is that he is a hypocrite. He pretends one thing but plots another. He speaks peace, but actually he is devising war.

Conclusion and Practical Advice

Yet enough of that! There will always be traitors and hypocrites and covenant breakers in this world. It is a fallen world. Righteousness you may hope for; sin you can count on. Sin is everywhere. The question is, What are the righteous to do in such deplorable conditions? Significantly, the psalm ends by answering this question. It tells us:

> Cast your cares on the LORD
> and he will sustain you;
> he will never let the righteous fall.

Psalm 55

But you, O God, will bring down the wicked
    into the pit of corruption;
bloodthirsty and deceitful men
    will not live out half their days.

But as for me, I trust in you.
verses 22–23

This statement is the verse picked up by the apostle Peter and commended to us in the fifth chapter of his first epistle: "Cast all your anxiety on him because he cares for you" (1 Peter 5:7). Early in his life Peter had been a very anxious person. In the final days of Jesus' earthly life Peter had been greatly worried about what might happen to Jesus, and then, when Jesus was arrested, he was even more worried about what might happen to himself. Peter was a great worrier, and not without cause. But as he grew older he learned not to worry but rather to do what he then also commended to other people, to cast his cares on God.

Why should we do that? Isn't this just another form of escapism, the kind of thing David was wanting to do early in Psalm 55? No. In fact, it is the exact opposite. It is learning to cast our cares on God that enables us not to run away but to stand tall and carry on with the task God has assigned us. Casting our cares on God enables us to be strong. The last verses give three reasons why we should cast our cares on the Lord.

1. *"He will sustain you."* When we are down it is natural to think that we will never be able to bear up under the troubles that are pressing in from every side. We are sure we will be beaten down. But that is not the case. The Bible says, "No temptation has seized you except what is common to man. And God is faithful; he will not let you be tempted beyond what

you can bear. But when you are tempted, he will also provide a way out so that you can stand up under it" (1 Cor. 10:13).

2. *"He will never let the righteous fall."* Peter was sure he was going to fall on one notable occasion. He was trying to walk toward Jesus over the water of the Sea of Galilee, looked at the waves, and began to sink. "Lord, save me!" he cried (Matt. 14:30). This is exactly what David has been praying in this psalm. He wanted to be saved. And the Lord did it. He saved David, just as he saved Peter and all who cast their cares upon him. David is not exaggerating when he says, "The LORD . . . will never let the righteous fall" (v. 22).

3. *"God . . . will bring down the wicked."* Evil people may succeed for a time, but it is the promise of God as well as the judgment of history that they soon perish and are destroyed, just as they had sought so hard to destroy other people.

The bottom line is the psalm's last sentence: "But as for me, I trust in you," that is, in God. That is David's final testimony. Is it yours? If you are focusing on the evil around you, you will not be able to say, "But as for me, I trust in you." But you will say it if you have really cast your cares on God.

Psalm 56

Be merciful to me, O God, for men hotly
        pursue me;
    all day long they press their attack.
My slanderers pursue me all day long;
    many are attacking me in their pride.

When I am afraid,
    I will trust in you.
In God, whose word I praise,
    in God I trust; I will not be afraid.
    What can mortal man do to me?

All day long they twist my words;
    they are always plotting to harm me.
They conspire, they lurk,
    they watch my steps,
    eager to take my life.

On no account let them escape;
    in your anger, O God, bring down the nations.
Record my lament;
    list my tears on your scroll—
    are they not in your record?

Then my enemies will turn back
    when I call for help.
    By this I will know that God is for me.

In God, whose word I praise,
    in the LORD, whose word I praise—
in God I trust; I will not be afraid.
    What can man do to me?

I am under vows to you, O God;
    I will present my thank offerings to you.
For you have delivered me from death
    and my feet from stumbling,
that I may walk before God
    in the light of life.

"What Can Man Do to Me?"

*W*hat can man do to me?

We do not have to think very long to come up with an answer to that: Man can do a lot to me! And to prove it, all we have to do is read the morning's newspaper. The week I wrote this chapter, on just one day I read these stories:

- An account of an attack on Serbian, Bulgarian, Rumanian, and Vietnamese refugees in Germany by neo-Nazis, while German police looked on. The refugees fought back and injured ten of their attackers.
- A United Nations vote to look into reports of war crimes by the Serbian government against Moslems in Bosnia. The Serbs were murdering thousands of Moslems in an offensive they call "ethnic cleansing."
- The trial of a man who sold an unsuspecting family a home with a defective gas heater, knowing it was dangerous. It emitted carbon monoxide, and the night it was first turned on three in the family, including an infant, were killed.
- The murder of a manager of a fast-food restaurant and the wounding of a coworker by two young thugs who wanted to rob them.

69

- The sentencing of two businessmen for insurance fraud.
- An abduction.
- Several cases of sexual abuse.

Sometimes I count the number of murders on a weekend in Philadelphia. Often there are up to half a dozen. But these are only the tip of the iceberg of evil in one city, a small, partial proof of what the nineteenth-century poet William Wordsworth once aptly called "man's inhumanity to man."

What can man do to me?

Man can oppress, slander, hurt, hate, maim, and murder me, for starters. But, of course, that is not the answer David is giving us in Psalm 56. His answer is, Nothing! Not if God is for me and stands against the opposition.

Into Death's Jaws

I suppose the immediate reaction to a statement like that is along these lines: "Well, that was easy for David to say. He was a king. He commanded an army. He lived in a fortified city. None of us are so lucky." I want you to see that this was not the situation in which David wrote the psalm. The title sets us straight on that. It tells us that it was written "when the Philistines had seized him in Gath."

Here is the story. When we were studying Psalm 52 we saw that early in his life David had been forced to escape from King Saul because Saul was trying to kill him. This was when David went to Nob, and this visit was later reported to King Saul by Doeg. I pointed out that there was a lapse of time between David's visit to Nob and Doeg's report to Saul. In fact, when we look this up in 1 Samuel 21–22, where the story is told, we find that two incidents filled this interval. The first was David's flight to the fortified Philistine city of Gath, where he thought he might be safe from Saul. The second occurred when he found he was not safe in Gath and escaped into the wilderness, to the cave at Adullam, where his brothers and other discontented people began to gather around him. At the end of this period David had collected about four hundred valiant men, who eventually became the core of his army.

Psalm 56 was written about David's time in Gath, so it is important to have this incident in full view in order to understand what is going on in the psalm. There are three things worth noting.

1. *David was alone.* He had fled from Saul without any soldiers, and even without food or weapons. We often think of him as having at least his four hundred valiant men with him when he was in the wilderness. We think of him having hearty companionship and at least some protection. But according to 1 Samuel 22, the gathering of his army occurred after the time in Gath. So David was entirely alone at this time. There was no one with him.

2. *David was desperate.* Gath had been the home of the giant Goliath, whom David had killed just a few years before. Goliath was a Philistine hero, and he had certainly been the pride of Gath. What except desperation would cause anyone to walk alone into the hometown of the hero he had killed?

And there is this, too, although I have not seen it mentioned in any of the commentaries. When David was at Nob only days before, he had asked Ahimelech if he had any weapons. Ahimelech gave him the only weapon he had, the sword of Goliath, which had been placed in Nob after David's victory. The sword is not described in the account of David's fight with Goliath in 1 Samuel 17. But the account says that Goliath was over nine feet tall and that his body armor and bronze javelin were unusually large and heavy. His sword must have been large too, and it was certainly remembered by the people of Gath and was easily recognized by them. There are only two ways any sane man would walk into Gath under those conditions: either in arrogant pride or in desperation. Since we know from the psalm that David was afraid rather than arrogant, he must have gone to Gath in near despair.

Derek Kidner begins his study by noting this: "To have fled from Saul to Gath of all places, the home town of Goliath, took the courage of despair; it measured David's estimate of his standing with his people." David's attempt to find safety in Gath was not successful, of course. Kidner adds, "This has failed, and [David] is [now] doubly encircled."[1]

3. *David was afraid.* We are told this explicitly in 1 Samuel. When David arrived in Gath, his presence was reported to the king of Gath, a man called Achish. The people told Achish,

> "Isn't this David, the king of the land? Isn't he the one they sing about in their dances:
>> "'Saul has slain his thousands,
>> and David his tens of thousands'?"

1 Samuel 21:11

Those "tens of thousands" were Philistines, and some of the former people of Gath as well as their hero Goliath were among them. Therefore, we are not surprised to read in the next sentence, "David took these words to heart and was very much afraid of Achish king of Gath" (v. 12). Since David had no one to defend him he resorted to cunning, pretending to be out of his mind so Achish would despise him rather than kill him. So he eventually escaped.

With this in mind we now read the central verses of the psalm:

> When I am afraid,
> I will trust in you.

∽ **Psalm 56** ∾

> In God, whose word I praise,
>   in God I trust; I will not be afraid.
> What can mortal man do to me?
>   verses 3–4

Do you ever feel afraid? Desperate? Alone? If so, this psalm is for you. You will find it to be encouraging, too, for it is not merely about loneliness and fear. It is about the faith that gives victory over those very real states and terrible emotions. I notice with approval that J. J. Stewart Perowne described the psalm as being about "the victory rather than the struggle of faith."[2]

But first, one more word about the title. It contains the notation "To the tune of 'A Dove on Distant Oaks.'" We know nothing about this tune, but the reference to a dove makes us think back to Psalm 55, in which David cried, "Oh, that I had the wings of a dove! I would fly away and be at rest" (v. 6). When we studied Psalm 55 we saw that David did not have the wings of a dove. But here we learn that he had something better. He had God who made the dove, and he found the peace he was seeking by trusting him.

Psalm 56 seems to have been popular with other biblical writers and is quoted elsewhere in Scripture. Verses 4 and 11 are picked up in Psalm 118:6 and quoted by the author of Hebrews in 13:6. Verse 9 is referred to by Paul in Romans 8:31. The first part of verse 13 is quoted in Psalm 116:8 with only slight alteration, and the last phrase, "the light of life," reappears in the third of Jesus' "I am" sayings in John's gospel: "I am the light of the world. Whoever follows me will never walk in darkness, but will have the light of life" (John 8:12).

The Outline

At this point in the Psalter we come to a number of psalms that have a repeating chorus. The next psalm, 57, is an example. The chorus is "Be exalted, O God, above the heavens; let your glory be over all the earth" (vv. 5, 11). Psalm 59 has the chorus "O my Strength, I watch for you; you, O God, are my fortress, my loving God" (vv. 9, 17).

I mention this here because the same pattern occurs in Psalm 56 and is the key to outlining it. In Psalm 56 the refrain is what I quoted earlier, calling it the "central" verse or verses of the psalm. It is found first in verse 4 and then a second time, slightly expanded, in verses 10 and 11. The psalm follows this pattern. First, there is a brief description of the trouble in which David finds himself (vv. 1–2). Second, there is a strong statement of faith, including the words of the chorus (vv. 3–4). Third, there is a further elaboration of the problem (vv. 5–9), followed, fourth, by a slightly expanded version of the chorus (vv. 10–11). Fifth, David promises to present a thanksgiving offering to God when he is saved by him (vv. 12–13).

The Voice of Fear

I wrote earlier of Psalm 56 being about "the victory rather than the struggle of faith" (Perowne). But that does not mean that fear is missing from the psalm. On the contrary, the fear described in 1 Samuel 21:12 is evident in the opening verses (vv. 1–2) and also in David's second, longer elaboration of the danger (vv. 5–9). There are two emphases.

1. *The fury of the attack.* Sometimes language can be used to capture the feeling of a moment, and that is the case in verses 1 and 2, where David conveys the relentless fury of his enemies' pursuit by striking word repetitions. There are three of them. "Pursue," "attack," and "all day long" are each repeated in verse 2 after being introduced first in verse 1. We read, "men hotly *pursue* me" and "my slanderers *pursue* me," "*all day long*" and "*all day long*," and finally "they press their *attack*" and "many

are *attacking* me." It is a striking way of saying, "I am over-whelmed, simply overwhelmed; because no matter what direction I turn they are always after me, after me, pursuing me, always pursuing me."

2. *The nature of the attack.* The second, later description of the problem (vv. 5–9) is not so furious. Rather it is a calmer description of the nature of the attacks being made. We might think from the setting that all David would be concerned about was his immediate physical danger. But even in verse 2 he spoke not merely of military attacks but of "slanderers," and now he explains that it is the slander that bothers him even more than the danger. They want to kill him, of course. But to justify their doing it (or perhaps to win the necessary numbers to their side) his enemies twist his words to make it seem that he is threatening the king:

> All day long they twist my words;
>   they are always plotting to harm me.
> They conspire, they lurk,
>   they watch my steps,
>   eager to take my life.
>
> verses 5–6

This section ends with a prayer that God will judge these enemies (v. 7) and with a request that God will remember his sorrows, making a list of them (v. 8). David is confident that God knows what he is going through and that he will remember it. In fact, he presents the tender concerns of God for himself and his people in an image that has been of immense comfort to generations of sorrowing believers. We know it best in the words of the King James Bible: "Put thou my tears in thy bottle." But the idea is much the same in the New International Version: "list my tears on your scroll" or "put my tears in your wineskin" (in footnote). The meaning is that

God will never forget nor ever be indifferent to the cares of any one of his much beloved people.

The Voice of Faith

I have already pointed out that the chorus, which occurs in verses 4, 10, and 11, is the very heart of the psalm. We have been invited to observe David's fear, but now in even clearer tones we hear the voice of faith:

> In God, whose word I praise,
>   in God I trust; I will not be afraid.
> What can mortal man do to me?
>   verse 4

And again, slightly expanded:

> In God, whose word I praise,
>   in the LORD, whose word I praise—
> in God I trust; I will not be afraid.
> What can man do to me?
>   verses 10–11

1. *Confidence in God.* In these verses there are two parts to David's confidence, and the first is that he is confident in God. He trusts God, whom he calls Elohim four times (two times in verse 4, once each in verses 10 and 11) and Jehovah once (in verse 10). He trusts—not man, not circumstances, not his own cunning, even though that was what he did at Gath— he trusts God: "In God I trust." It is because of this that he can ask, "What can man do to me?" and expect the answer: Nothing!

So let me ask, Do you trust God? If you are a Christian, you have trusted him in the matter of your salvation. That is the greatest thing. God has saved you from sin, hell, and the devil. If God has done that, can you not also trust him in lesser things like loneliness or even those sometimes dangerous circumstances that cause fear and desperation? The Bible teaches that God will take care of you if you belong to him and are following after Jesus Christ. David wrote in an earlier psalm, "I was young and now I am old, yet I have never seen the righteous forsaken or their children begging bread" (Ps. 37:25). The psalm immediately before this one argued, "Cast your cares on the LORD and he will sustain you" (Ps. 55:22). The apostle Paul wrote to the Philippians, "My God will meet all your needs according to his glorious riches in Christ Jesus" (Phil. 4:19).

2. *Confidence in the Word of God.* There is another aspect to David's confidence in God: It is also based on the Word of God. Certainly you have noticed in the words of this repeated chorus that the phrase "whose word I praise" occurs three times. This is very important, because apart from the Word of God we do not know what God is like, and we certainly do not know what he has promised to do for us. What is this "word of God" to which David refers? Clearly it is the entire self-revelation of God in Scripture given up to that time. In other words, it is the Pentateuch (the first five books) and possibly Joshua and Judges. That is only a portion of our Bible, but it was enough to make God's character and desires for his people known. In the chorus of Psalm 56 David therefore praises God for his Word, recognizing it as one of the greatest of all God's good gifts to men and women.

It may also be the case, however, that David is thinking specifically of the words of God that were brought to him by the prophet Samuel, assuring him that he would be king over Israel (cf. 1 Sam. 16:1–13). That must have seemed a long way off when David was in Gath or hiding in the cave of Adul-

lam. But no matter! It was the Word of God, and though the
fulfillment of that Word might be long delayed it was nevertheless absolutely certain. Therefore, it was not only in God
but also in the specific words of God that David trusted.

You and I do not have individualized revelations from God
delivered to us today by God's prophets. We have the Bible.
But the Bible we have is more extensive than David's. It contains all we need to know about spiritual things. Equally important, we have the Holy Spirit to give us understanding of what
has been written as well as the ability to apply it to specific
areas of our lives.

New Life in Christ

The last two verses of Psalm 56, verses 12 and 13, are like
the ending of Psalm 54, in which David vows to present a
thanksgiving offering to God when he is delivered, so certain
is he that God will deliver him in time:

> I am under vows to you, O God;
>   I will present my thank offerings to you.
> For you have delivered me from death
>   and my feet from stumbling,
> that I may walk before God
>   in the light of life.

This is a great vow of confidence, like the confidence of
Psalm 34, which is also based on the incident at Gath. David
got this confidence by praying, and so can we. Confidence
comes to the person who prays and trusts God.

I want you to see one thing more before I end this study.
The fact that Jesus seems to have used the last words of verse
13 in John 8:12 makes us think of verse 13 in light of the deliverance Jesus brings to those who trust him and the "life" as

his gift of salvation by the Holy Spirit. That is the ultimate fulfillment of the psalm, of course. As Alexander Maclaren says, "The really living are they who live in Jesus, and the real light of the living is the sunshine that streams on those who thus live, because they live in him."[3] So I end this way. If you really want to move out from your fear, despair, and loneliness to bask in God's sunshine, live looking upward always into the face of Jesus Christ. Then you will find yourself saying firmly, "In God I trust; I will not be afraid. What can man do to me?"

Psalm

57

Have mercy on me, O God, have mercy
    on me,
  for in you my soul takes refuge.
I will take refuge in the shadow of your wings
  until the disaster has passed.

I cry out to God Most High,
  to God, who fulfills his purpose for me.
He sends from heaven and saves me,
  rebuking those who hotly pursue me;   *Selah*
  God sends his love and his faithfulness.

I am in the midst of lions;
  I lie among ravenous beasts—
men whose teeth are spears and arrows,
  whose tongues are sharp swords.

Be exalted, O God, above the heavens;
  let your glory be over all the earth.
They spread a net for my feet—
  I was bowed down in distress.
 They dug a pit in my path—
  but they have fallen into it themselves. *Selah*

My heart is steadfast, O God,
  my heart is steadfast;
  I will sing and make music.
Awake, my soul!
  Awake, harp and lyre!
  I will awaken the dawn.

I will praise you, O Lord, among the nations;
    I will sing of you among the peoples.
For great is your love, reaching to the heavens;
    your faithfulness reaches to the skies.

Be exalted, O God, above the heavens;
    let your glory be over all the earth.

Hiding in Thee

For several chapters we have been looking at psalms that are linked to that early desperate period of David's life when he was forced to flee into the wilderness from King Saul, who wanted to kill him. Psalm 52 began this set of psalms. Psalm 54 is another such psalm. Worst of all, Psalm 56 describes David's desperate plight in the Philistine town of Gath, to which he went alone, desperate, and afraid.

After David left Gath he faded into the wilderness and hid in a large cave known as Adullam, to which the title of Psalm 57 ("When he had fled from Saul into the cave") probably refers.[1] David was also alone there, at least at the beginning. But this was a turning point in his fortunes. First Samuel 22 tells us that it was while he was at Adullam that his brothers and his father's household and all who were in distress or debt or discontented began to gather around him. In all about four hundred men came to him, and he became their leader. Although there is nothing in Psalm 57 to indicate that this had begun to happen by the time the psalm was written, there is nevertheless a very noticeable change in the tone of the composition. The earlier psalms were mostly uncertain, fearful, even desperate. Psalm 57 is settled, and its prevailing note is praise.

What makes the difference?

In the earlier psalms David was hiding *from his enemies*—in Gath or in the wilderness of the Ziphites. Here he is hiding *in God*, which is what the cave comes to symbolize. David sings a great song in Psalm 57. It's something like our contemporary hymn "Hiding in Thee."

> O safe to the Rock that is higher than I
> My soul in its conflicts and sorrows would fly;
> So sinful, so weary, thine, thine would I be;
> Thou blest Rock of Ages, I'm hiding in thee.
> Hiding in thee, hiding in thee—
> Thou blest Rock of Ages, I'm hiding in thee.

Hiding in thee is what Psalm 57 is about.

The Psalm and Its Outline

How should the psalm be outlined? The psalm's eleven verses could be divided into three parts: (1) a call to God for mercy (vv. 1–3), (2) a description of the problem that caused David to ask for mercy (vv. 4–6), and (3) concluding praise of God (vv. 7–11). But in view of the refrain, which is repeated in verses 5 and 11, it is best to take the psalm in two main parts, each ending with the refrain. This is the outline suggested by J. J. Stewart Perowne and by H. C. Leupold, who says, "The first section, vv. 1–5, is a confident cry for deliverance from cruel enemies; the second section, vv. 6–11, is a resolve to praise God for deliverance."[2]

Verses 7 through 11 appear again as the opening verses of Psalm 108 (the second half of Psalm 108 is borrowed from Psalm 60:5–12), and a number of phrases echo words, verses, and images found in other places.[3]

Part One: Safe in God's Shadow

The first of the psalm's two parts begins with David asking for mercy even as he takes refuge in God. Since the title of the psalm speaks of the cave in which David was hiding it is natural to think that the cave suggested the idea of a refuge. But we should notice that David does not call the cave his refuge, though it was a refuge in a certain physical sense. Rather it is God whom he calls his refuge. Indeed, to use the image of the second half of verse 1, although David may have been hidden physically in the dark shadows of the vast cave of Adullam, he knows that it is actually under the shadow of the wings of God that he has found safety. That is the only place any of us are really safe.

Here is the point to notice how prominent God is in this psalm and thus also in the mind of the young fugitive. In this psalm God is referred to twenty-one times either by name or pronoun, and there are other words and phrases like "refuge" and "shadow of your wings" that refer to him as well. "Shadow of your wings" is a particularly rich image, and Bible students have looked at it in two ways.

1. *The wings of the cherubim.* The most frequent Old Testament use of the word *wings* is to refer to the wings of the golden cherubim that were on the lid of the ark of the covenant in the Most Holy Place of the temple or tabernacle. They are mentioned first in Exodus 25:17–20: "Make an atonement cover of pure gold—two and a half cubits long and a cubit and a half wide. And make two cherubim out of hammered gold at the ends of the cover. Make one cherub on one end and the second cherub on the other; make the cherubim of one piece with the cover, at the two ends. The cherubim are to have their wings spread upward, overshadowing the cover with them. The cherubim are to face each other, looking

toward the cover." This description occurs again in Exodus 37:9 and 1 Kings 6:27, and there are additional references to the cherubim's wings in 1 Kings 8:6–7, 1 Chronicles 28:18, and 2 Chronicles 3:13 and 5:7–8. Apparently Ezekiel in his visions of heaven saw the heavenly beings of which the golden cherubim were representations, and in that book the word *wings* occurs more than twenty times. There is a similar vision and reference in Revelation 4:8.

The tabernacle and its divinely appointed articles of furniture were so prominent in the religious outlook of the Jewish people that it is easy to suppose that David might have been thinking of the wings of the cherubim here, especially since the wings of the temple cherubim encompassed the space where God was supposed to dwell. If this is what is intended, David would be saying that he is as secure as if he were himself within the Most Holy Place, next to or virtually one with God.

The difficulty, of course, is that Psalm 57:1 does not speak of the wings of the cherubim, however significant they may have been, but of "your wings," which means the wings of God. It is much more natural therefore to think along the lines of Jesus' use of the image in Matthew 23, where he said, "O Jerusalem, Jerusalem, you who kill the prophets and stone those sent to you, how often I have longed to gather your children together, as a hen gathers her chicks under her wings, but you were not willing" (v. 37; cf. Luke 13:34). This is not the most natural image with which we might think of God, but it was probably quite a bit more natural for these ancient Jews. It leads to the second possibility.

2. *The wings of God.* The problem with the first image has led other commentators to explain David's reference as to the wings of God himself. To the objection that God does not have wings or that the image is unworthy of the Almighty we answer

that God speaks along these lines himself in several places. Indeed, the earliest biblical use of the word *wings* is an example. In Exodus 19:4, God declares, "You yourselves have seen what I did to Egypt, and how I carried you on eagles' wings and brought you to myself." This initial use of the image later lends itself to several variations. Thus, in the Song of Moses God is compared to

> an eagle that stirs up its nest
>   and hovers over its young,
> that spreads its wings to catch them
>   and carries them on its pinions.
>   Deuteronomy 32:11

The phrase "*shadow* of your wings," occurring in Psalm 57:1, is also in Psalms 17:8, 36:7, 61:4, and 63:7. In Psalm 91:1 the phrase becomes "shadow of the Almighty," and verse 4 of that psalm says, in words that are very close to Psalm 57:

> He will cover you with his feathers,
>   and under his wings you will find refuge;
>   his faithfulness will be your shield and rampart.

In the second stanza of part one (vv. 2–3) David refers to God as "God Most High." This name occurs in the Bible first in the story of Abraham and Melchizedek, where Abraham presents offerings to this otherwise unknown king of Salem. Melchizedek blesses Abraham by "God Most High, Creator of heaven and earth . . . who delivered your enemies into your hand" (Gen. 14:19–20). Derek Kidner thinks this name is intended to draw attention to Abraham as "another homeless man."[4] But in David's situation it is more likely that it is chosen for the sake of the accompanying phrase "who delivered your enemies into your hand." This is what David needed (as well as being delivered from his enemies), and it is what God did. First God delivered David. Then he delivered Saul, David's chief enemy, into David's hand. He did it more than once (cf. 1 Sam. 24, 26).

In these desperate early days, wherever David went he seemed to be "in the midst of lions" (v. 4). But when he lay down in the cave of Adullam "in the shadow of [God's] wings," he was as safe as Daniel in the lion's den. Daniel had been thrown to the lions for execution, but God protected him by closing the lions' mouths. He was never safer than when he had the lions around him to protect him. Who would dare even to come close? If Daniel had lived before David and if David had known Daniel's words, David might well have used them to tell Saul, "My God sent his angel, and he shut the mouths of the lions. They have not hurt me, because I was found innocent in his sight. Nor have I ever done any wrong before you, O king" (Dan. 6:22).

Part Two: A Heightened Testimony

I want to deal now with part two of this psalm, holding consideration of the refrain for last, as I did with Psalm 56.

Generally speaking, part two has the same themes as part one. But we need to see how they are introduced and what happens to them the second time around. Seeing this will help us to understand something about Hebrew poetry. First, we need to look at the general subject matter of the three stanzas in part one. Verse 1 is the first. It is an appeal to God for mercy, coupled with a resolute determination to take refuge in him. Verses 2 and 3 are the second stanza. They are a testimony to God's faithfulness to David. Verse 4 is the third stanza, the last of part one, apart from the chorus. It is a description of David's enemies and of the danger he is in because of them.

Now look at part two. These same general themes occur there, only in inverse order. The first stanza is verse 6. It deals with David's enemies, which is what the third stanza (v. 4) did in part one. The second stanza is composed of verses 7 and 8. It also deals with faithfulness or steadfastness, as the second stanza of part one did, only here the steadfastness is David's. Because God is faithful, David will also be faithful and will sing praises to him. The third stanza, verses 9 and 10, is like the first in part one (v. 1) in that it is another cry to God. So the structure of the psalm is:

A, B, C / chorus
C, B, A / chorus

But notice this. The second time around the intensity of each of the three themes is raised a notch or two higher, and the tone of the psalm becomes gloriously strong and confident, all because the psalmist is focusing on God primarily—he is hiding in God, after all—and not on his problems.

The stanzas that I have identified as "C" deal with David's enemies, but the description of danger that is found in the first part gives way to the confidence that the pit they have dug for David will trap them. They will fall into it themselves.

The stanzas that I have identified as "B" deal with David's relationship to God. But the earlier expression of confidence, which is already on a very high note, rises even higher as David moves from confidence in God to actual singing, so wonderful does God seem to him.

> My heart is steadfast;
> I will sing and make music. . . .

∽ **Psalm 57** ∾

Awake, harp and lyre!
I will awaken the dawn.
verses 7–8

The stanzas that I have identified as "A" are direct addresses to God. The appeal for mercy in part one rises to pure praise in part two:

I will praise you, O Lord, among the nations;
I will sing of you among the peoples.
For great is your love, reaching to the heavens;
your faithfulness reaches to the skies.
verses 9–10

This is not the first occurrence of the words *love* and *faithfulness* in this psalm. They are found first in verse 3, at the beginning, and now also here in verse 10, at the end. In between we have David's believing declaration "My heart is steadfast," repeated twice for emphasis (a Hebrew poetic device). Because God is faithful, David will be faithful. This makes verse 7 the emotional focal point of the psalm.

So I apply the psalm here, asking, Are you faithful in this sense? Is your heart steadfast?

Alexander Maclaren preached a sermon on this verse titled "The Fixed Heart" in which he provided some wise words and asked some searching questions:

For a fixed heart I must have a fixed determination and not a mere fluctuating and soon broken intention. I must have a steadfast affection, and not merely a fluttering love that, like some butterfly, lights now on this, now on that sweet flower, but which has a flight straight as a carrier pigeon to its cot, which shall bear me direct to God. And I must have a continuous realization of my dependence upon God and of God's sweet sufficiency going with me all through the dusty day. . . .

Ah, brethren! How unlike the broken, interrupted, divergent lines that we draw! . . . Is our average Christianity fairly represented by such words as these of my text? Do they not rather make us burn with shame when we think that a man who lived in the twilight of God's revelation, and was weighed upon by distresses such as wrung this psalm out of him, should have poured out this resolve, which we who live in the sunlight and are flooded with blessings find it hard to echo with sincerity and truth?

Fixed hearts are rare amongst the Christians of this day.[5]

Maclaren died more than fifty years ago, about the time I was born. But who would argue that the situation has improved even a trifle in the last half century? People do not have fixed hearts in their closest, most intimate relationships. They break friendships, even marriages easily. They do not have fixed hearts in regard to their work. There is very little employer-employee loyalty. They do not even have fixed hearts in the work of God, for they abandon their responsibilities and drop out easily.

To God Be the Glory

After what we have seen so far in this psalm we are not surprised to find the chorus calling for God to be exalted: "Be exalted, O God, above the heavens; let your glory be over all the earth" (vv. 5, 11). God is exalted above the heavens. His glory does fill the earth. The goal of history is that God might be known as God and be honored for it. Nothing will frustrate this worthy purpose of the Almighty.

But this repeated chorus is not a statement that God has been or will be exalted. It is a prayer that he might be exalted. And that raises the questions: How so? In what manner? And by whom? The answer to those questions is that David wants God to be exalted in his own circumstances and by the way he trusts and praises God even in difficulties.

This makes me think of something in the Book of Ephesians. In the third chapter Paul is writing of the glory of what God is accomplishing in the church in which Jews and Gentiles are being brought together into one body and in which even their sufferings demonstrate the sufficiency of God in all circumstances. He has been speaking of this for several chapters, but here he takes it up an octave, arguing that even the angels marvel at this manifestation of God's wisdom:

> His intent was that now, through the church, the manifold wisdom of God should be made known to the rulers and authorities in the heavenly realms, according to his eternal purpose which he accomplished in Christ Jesus our Lord. In him and through faith in him we may approach God with freedom and confidence. I ask you, therefore, not to be discouraged because of my sufferings for you, which are your glory.
>
> Ephesians 3:10–13

This is exactly what David is saying in Psalm 57. The world thrills when human beings are exalted. It fawns on kings, rulers, and statesmen, the rich and the famous. But those who know God rejoice when God is exalted, and they rejoice that they have the great privilege of exalting him themselves, especially in circumstances that are disappointing or hard.

Psalm 58

Do you rulers indeed speak justly?
  Do you judge uprightly among men?
No, in your heart you devise injustice,
    and your hands mete out violence on the
      earth.
Even from birth the wicked go astray;
    from the womb they are wayward and speak
      lies.

Their venom is like the venom of a snake,
    like that of a cobra that has stopped its ears,
that will not heed the tune of the charmer,
    however skillful the enchanter may be.

Break the teeth in their mouths, O God;
    tear out, O Lord, the fangs of the lions!
Let them vanish like water that flows away;
    when they draw the bow, let their arrows be
      blunted.
Like a slug melting away as it moves along,
    like a stillborn child, may they not see the
      sun.

Before your pots can feel the heat of the
      thorns—
    whether they be green or dry—the wicked
    will be swept away.
The righteous will be glad when they are
      avenged,

when they bathe their feet in the blood of
    the wicked.
Then men will say,
    "Surely the righteous still are rewarded;
    surely there is a God who judges the earth."

Low Deeds in High Places

*T*here was a time in American political history when anyone reading Psalm 58 would have thought it somehow unreal, at least where the United States is concerned. Psalm 58 is about unjust rulers, and in those earlier halcyon days America was favored for the most part with leaders whose characters were upright and whose actions were above reproach. No longer. Today corruption is widespread even at the highest levels of political leadership, and Psalm 58 seems to be an apt prophetic description of our times.

Even secular observers see it. Speaking of our national life, the *Washington Post* said recently that "common decency can no longer be described as common." The *New Republic* magazine declared, "There is a destructive sense that nothing is true and everything is permitted."[1]

On April 4, 1991, Charles W. Colson gave an address on ethics at the Harvard Business School. Not long before this the school had established a Chair on Ethics, recognizing that the moral decline of American leadership is a significant social problem, and Colson had objected that "Harvard's philosophical relativism precludes the teaching of ethics." Now he was invited to address this intelligent and

95

highly critical body. He expected the worst. Only a few years earlier the Nobel prize–winning neurobiologist Sir John Eccles had been booed when he had suggested that although we can account for brain cells through evolution, the consciousness of the mind is something that has to have come from God. Nevertheless, when Colson reviewed the recent moral scandals involving America's leadership, he received a respectful hearing.

He spoke of the Keating Five, five United States senators tried, in effect, by their own tribunal for complicity in the savings and loan scandal; Senator Dave Durenberger, who was censured by the Senate; Marion Barry, the mayor of the District of Columbia, arrested for drug use; congressmen who have been turned out of office by the scores; and, perhaps most reprehensible of all, the HUD scandal, in which people were ripping off large sums of money from funds designed by law to help the poor.

Colson referred to a press release in which the Department of Justice boasted that in 1990 they had prosecuted *and convicted* 1,500 public officials, the highest number in the history of the country. They were boasting about it![2] It was a sad commentary on the corruption that has become epidemic in contemporary American life, corruption that the business school students seemed to recognize, even though they did not know what to do about it.

A Vigorous Protest

The audience that heard Colson's address was mostly passive, however, as many Americans seem to be today. Americans tend to dismiss corruption, saying simply, "Well, that's just the way people are." And they are, of course! That is what original sin is all about. G. K. Chesterton said that the doctrine of original sin is the only philosophy that has been empirically validated by 3,500 years of human history. But the fact that "all have sinned" and that low deeds in high places are so frequent does not mean that we are to accept sin or corruption passively, especially in our leaders—or in ourselves!

David did not accept sin passively, either here or elsewhere. On the contrary, Psalm 58 is a particularly vigorous protest against the evil he saw in ancient Israel at least a thousand years before the birth of Jesus Christ.

J. J. Stewart Perowne says, "This psalm is a bold protest against unrighteous judges. It opens with an indignant expostulation on their deliberate perversion of justice, whilst they pretend to uphold it. It lays bare their character and that of those whom they favor, as men thoroughly, habitually, by their very nature, corrupt. And finally, because they are thus beyond all hope of correction or amendment, it calls upon God to rob them of their power and to bring all their counsels to nought."[3]

Psalm 58 is an imprecatory psalm—that is, a psalm in which the writer calls on God to judge the ungodly, in this case the unjust judges. Many people are disturbed by these psalms because they consider them to be vindictive. They point out that we have been told by Jesus to forgive our enemies and pray for God to bless them rather than punish them. This is true, but it is not the whole truth. For one thing, the imprecatory psalms do not express hatred of others or even a desire for revenge on the part of the writer but only the desire that God would intervene in history to judge the worst sins of the worst men and thereby permit righteousness to flourish. It is a matter of the writer siding with God and his righteousness, and not with evil.

The imprecatory psalms have another function too, and that is to remind us to make sure we are not like those who are being faulted for their evil. The people described in this psalm are habitual offenders, people who are impervious to correction. As we study the psalm we should make sure that we are not like them, that our sin is covered by the blood of Jesus Christ, and that God has given us ears to hear what the Holy Spirit of correction says to us about our own evil ways.

A Description of the Wicked

The stanzas of the New International Version are a reasonable way to outline this psalm. The first stanza is itself in two parts, since verses 1 and 2 address the wicked directly while verses 3 through 5 describe what they are like. But there is a sense in which the entire stanza is a portrait of these people. Stanza two is a prayer that they might be overcome or destroyed, a malediction. It occupies verses 6 through 8. The final stanza, verses 9 through 11, is a prediction of the end of the wicked and the vindication of the righteous. It concludes with a striking summary in verse 11.

The opening verses, then, are a rebuke of the corrupt rulers of David's day. They are addressed directly, and they are accused of failing to do the one thing they are appointed to do, which is to speak and judge justly.

There are problems with the text, which we can easily see by comparing the English translations. What I have just said is clear in any translation, but there is a problem with the Hebrew word the New International Version translates as *rulers* (v. 1). The word is *elem*, which means muteness or silence. It is hard to fit this word and its form into the text, but the older versions do the best they can and come up with something like the New King James Version, which says, "Do you indeed speak righteousness, you silent ones?" But because the word is close in form in Hebrew to the word *elohim*, which means gods and is also used in the sense of "mighty ones" or "rulers" in the psalms, some of the more recent versions take it as referring to the judges themselves. So we have translations like the New International Version: "Do you rulers indeed speak justly?"

I am not sure that it is possible to reach certainty about how the text should be taken. But I tend to stick with how the text actually reads and avoid emendations, however reasonable, and if that is right, then the problem is that these judges did not speak up for the right course of action when evil was being planned. Perowne says, "They are *dumb* when they ought to speak, as afterwards they are said to be *deaf* when they ought to hear."[4] The next sentences show that these evil persons also plotted evil and put it into practice. But if *silence* is the right translation in verse 1, then the opening stanza accuses them of silence and reminds us that to remain silent when evil is planned is also an evil and deserves God's condemnation.

Are you careful to stand up for righteousness when evil is proposed and good is challenged? Remember that a courageous, good word can be extremely effective. It is not always successful, but it can be; and in any case, we need to speak up for what is right. It was because of the protest of one righteous man, Ebed-Melech, a Cushite, that the prophet Jeremiah was saved when his enemies had thrown him into a cistern to die (cf. Jer. 38:1–13). If Ebed-Melech had not defended him, Jeremiah would have perished.

Verses 3 through 5 add two damaging accusations to the charge against the unjust judges or rulers.

1. *They are evil from birth (v. 3).* David is thinking of this special class of evildoers, as opposed to occasional wrongdoers or the righteous. But we should remember that this is also an accurate description of all men and women in their natural state. No one is born righteous. We are born sinners. In fact, it is because we are born sinners that we sin. Even David said, "Surely I was sinful at birth, sinful from the time my mother

conceived me" (Ps. 51:5). He meant that there was never a moment of his life, even from his conception, when he did not possess a sinful nature. It is because we are sinners that we need a Savior.

2. *They will not listen to appeals to act differently (vv. 4–5).* Psalm 58 is noteworthy for its striking images, and one of these is its description of evildoers as snakes. This is not an uncommon image with us, as we also might call some particularly devious person a snake, but here David calls attention to the snake's venom or poison. The snake's bite kills. Then he adds an additional striking thought, describing these persons as snakes that cannot hear and therefore cannot even be controlled by the tunes of the snake charmer. I am told that snakes do not actually hear very much, if anything. They are controlled more by the motion of the flute than by the tune. But that is irrelevant to the writer's image. His point is that people intent on evil will not listen to those trying to dissuade them, either man or God. Therefore, they are equally deaf both to reason and to revelation.

God told Ezekiel, "Son of man, you are living among a rebellious people. They have eyes to see but do not see and ears to hear but do not hear, for they are a rebellious people" (Ezek. 12:2). Isaiah said, "You have seen many things, but have paid no attention; your ears are open, but you hear nothing" (Is. 42:20). That is true of all of us in our natural state. Therefore, if we are to hear anything God says, we must have our ears opened by the Holy Spirit. Paul wrote, "The man without the Spirit does not accept the things that come from the Spirit of God, for they are foolishness to him, and he cannot understand them, because they are spiritually discerned" (1 Cor. 2:14). John wrote in Revelation, "He who has an ear [that is, given by the Holy Spirit], let him hear what the Spirit says to the churches" (Rev. 2:11).

A Prayer against the Wicked

The second stanza of Psalm 58 moves from a description of the wicked to a prayer that they and their evil might be overthrown by God. It contains five images for what David is asking God to do. They move from what is powerful to what is increasingly weak, from what is awe inspiring to what is merely tragic or sad.

1. *The teeth of a lion.* The most awe-inspiring image is that of a lion that is fierce and able to kill and do great damage. David had used the image earlier, in the psalm immediately preceding this one, where he described himself as being "in the midst of lions . . . among ravenous beasts" (Ps. 57:4). Here he is asking God to defang his fierce enemies, to break the teeth of those who would consume him. God did this when he caused the armies of Saul to be defeated by the Philistines in the battle that preceded the call of David to be king.

2. *Water that flows away.* Water can be very destructive in large quantities, as in a flood. It can wash away houses, even whole villages, and claim lives. But it is also a characteristic of water that it flows downhill and therefore quickly drains away and vanishes. David uses this image to ask that God will cause the workers of evil to pass by quickly and vanish into the earth like water into parched soil.

3. *Blunted arrows.* Arrows are less destructive than masses of water, but in the hands of a skilled archer they can wound and kill. David has used this image in the previous psalm too, describing his enemies as "men whose teeth are spears and arrows" (Ps. 57:4). He knew the piercing, wounding, killing power of evil words. But God can blunt words' effects. David knew that. So he prays in these verses, "When they draw the bow, let their arrows be blunted" (v. 7). At the time of Absalom's rebellion against his father, David prayed that the wise

counsel of Ahithophel might fall on deaf ears and so be disregarded. It was. Absalom listened to Hushai instead of Ahithophel and eventually lost the war (cf. 2 Sam. 16–17).

4. *A melting slug.* A slug does not actually melt away as it moves along the ground leaving its slimy trail behind. But it seems to, and it is this image that David creates to describe the self-consuming pathway of the wicked. As Alexander Maclaren says, "Opposition to God's will destroys itself by its own activity."[5] David expressed the same thought in Psalm 57 when he said by another image, "They dug a pit in my path— but they have fallen into it themselves" (v. 6).

5. *A stillborn child.* The last image is of a child born dead, what we call a still birth. So it is David's prayer that the lives of these evil ones might be nipped at the beginning. This image corresponds closely to his statement in verse 3 that the wicked have gone astray "from birth." His thinking is that if they have been evil from birth, they should be cut off at birth.

It's God's World after All

Psalm 58 reaches its climax in the last stanza with a prophecy, a confident statement that the wicked will be judged by God and the righteous rewarded. The moral is that although judgment may tarry long, it will come, and when it comes, the way of the righteous will be seen to have been right.

But there is a problem with verse 9. I wrote earlier that translators cannot agree on the meaning of verse 1 because of the word *silent.* Those problems are increased manyfold in this verse, because there are several words for which the meaning is unclear. The word translated as *pots* (NIV) can mean either a pot used for cooking or a thorn. The word rendered *green,* as in wood that has not yet dried out, can also mean raw as in raw or uncooked meat. The words *the heat of* have been added, meaning that the text actually says only "feel the thorns." There are a few other more minor problems too. If you compare Bible translations, you can see at once how these cause the translations to differ.[6]

On the other hand, in spite of these problems of translation the general meaning is clear. As Alexander Maclaren says, "It is a homely and therefore vigorous picture of half-accomplished plans suddenly reduced to utter failure, and leaving their concocters hungry for the satisfaction which seemed so near."[7]

I wrote earlier that the climax of the psalm comes in the moral of verse 11—that although judgment may tarry long, it will come, and when it comes, the way of the righteous will be seen to have been right:

> Then men will say,
>   "Surely the righteous still are rewarded;
>   surely there is a God who judges the earth."

That is something worth remembering. We tend to forget that it is true, especially when we see evil winning out for a time, as evil often does. But those who fix their eyes on God and believe God and his Word will remember it. They will have a long-range perspective and will live accordingly. They will do right and stand for righteousness, knowing that evil will be judged and good rewarded in the end.

The title of this psalm calls it a *miktam*. No one is entirely sure what this means, which is why it appears as *miktam* rather than being translated. But the word seems to have its root in a verb meaning to engrave, and this seems to have been the understanding of the translators of the Septuagint version, since they rendered it by *stêlographia,* which means an inscription on a stele or column. Noting this, John Jebb, writing in 1846, had this suggestion: "It appears by the titles of four out of these six psalms, that they were composed by David while fleeing and hiding from the persecutions of Saul. What, then, should hinder us from imagining that they were inscribed on the rocks and on the sides of the caves which so often formed his place of refuge? This view would accord with the strict etymological meaning of the word, and explain the rendering of the Septuagint."[8]

I do not know whether that is a correct explanation of the use of this word in the titles of these psalms. But whether or not these words were inscribed on the rock walls of the cave of Adullam, let them be inscribed on your heart. Let this climactic saying be a *miktam* to you. Assure yourself on the basis of God's revelation in the Bible that "the righteous still are rewarded" and that "there is a God who judges the earth."

And equally important, make sure that you live for him and stand for righteousness. You cannot do it by yourself. But you can do it by the power of Christ who lives in you, if you are a Christian.

I began this study by citing some things Charles Colson said to students in the Harvard Business School in 1991. I return to what he said now, because he ended his speech on this note, speaking personally:

> Even the most rational approach to ethics is defenseless if there isn't the will to do what is right. On my own—and I can only speak for myself—I do not have that will. That which I want to do, I do not; that which I do, I do not want to do.
>
> It is only when I can turn to the One whom we celebrate at Easter—the One who was raised from the dead—that I can find the will to do what is right. It's only when that value and that sense of righteousness pervade a society that there can be a moral consensus. I would hope I might leave you, as future business leaders, the thought that a society

of which we are a part—and for which you should have a great sense of responsibility and stewardship—desperately needs those kind of values. And, if I might say so, each one of us does as well.[9]

I hope you know what Charles Colson found out about himself—that apart from God there is no limit to the evil of which you are capable, but that in Jesus Christ you can have not only forgiveness of sins but also the will and motivation to live differently.

Psalm 58

Psalm 59

Deliver me from my enemies, O God;
    protect me from those who rise up against me.
Deliver me from evildoers
    and save me from bloodthirsty men.

See how they lie in wait for me!
    Fierce men conspire against me
    for no offense or sin of mine, O LORD.
I have done no wrong, yet they are ready
        to attack me.
    Arise to help me; look on my plight!
O LORD God Almighty, the God of Israel,
    rouse yourself to punish all the nations;
    show no mercy to wicked traitors.   *Selah*

They return at evening,
    snarling like dogs,
    and prowl about the city.
See what they spew from their mouths—
    they spew out swords from their lips,
    and they say, "Who can hear us?"
But you, O LORD, laugh at them;
    you scoff at those nations.

O my Strength, I watch for you;
    you, O God, are my fortress,
        my loving God.

God will go before me
 and will let me gloat over those who
  slander me.
But do not kill them, O Lord our shield,
 or my people will forget.
In your might make them wander about,
 and bring them down.
For the sins of their mouths,
 for the words of their lips,
 let them be caught in their pride.
For the curses and lies they utter,
 consume them in wrath,
 consume them till they are no more.
Then it will be known to the ends of the earth
 that God rules over Jacob.   *Selah*

They return at evening,
 snarling like dogs,
 and prowl about the city.
They wander about for food
 and howl if not satisfied.
But I will sing of your strength,
 in the morning I will sing of your love;
for you are my fortress,
 my refuge in times of trouble.

O my Strength, I sing praise to you;
 you, O God, are my fortress,
  my loving God.

God Is My Fortress

*P*salm 59 is another psalm with a historical setting from the life of David, the great poet of the first two books of psalms. These historically based psalms have appeared in more or less alternating order since Psalm 51. That is, when we look at the titles of these psalms, we find historical references for Psalms 51, 52, 54, 56, 57, and now 59 and 60. Most of these are linked to the days when David was hiding from King Saul, first at Nob, then at Gath, next in the wilderness of Ziph, and finally in the wilderness cave of Adullam. As the collection comes to an end, we find Psalm 60 looking ahead to something that happened later in David's life when he had been king for some time, and Psalm 59, which we are to study now, looking back to David's first troubles with the king. The order is not chronological, but it suggests that there is no time in our lives when we will be without troubles.

Psalm 59 is about the time "when Saul had sent men to watch David's house in order to kill him." The story is in 1 Samuel 19:11–18.

David's Escape

David was still with Saul in those days. But it was the time following David's victory over Goliath, and the women of Israel had been singing, "Saul has slain his thousands, and David his tens of thousands" (1 Sam. 18:7), and Saul was jealous. Twice he became so distraught that he threw his spear at David (1 Sam. 18:10–11; 19:9–10), but each time David escaped. After the second attempt on his life David thought it would be wise to leave Saul and his court and go to his own home, but that night the king sent soldiers to surround David's house, watch it, and kill him in the morning. David was married to Saul's daughter Michal at this time. She loved David and warned him, "If you don't run for your life tonight, tomorrow you'll be killed" (1 Sam. 19:11). Michal seems to have known her father well, just as her brother Jonathan, David's friend, also did. So that night Michal let David down through a window of the house, presumably outside the city's walls or into a back alley, and he escaped.

Michal also bought David time. She put an idol in his bed, covered it with a blanket, and set some goat's hair at its head. When the soldiers came in the next morning, it looked as if David was asleep. "He is ill," Michal said. The soldiers reported this to Saul. Saul told them to bring David to him on the bed so he could kill him anyway. But when the soldiers went back to David's house and discovered the ruse, David was long gone.

This is the historical setting for the psalm, and the psalm is quite understandable against this background.[1] There are a few phrases, however, that suggest that it may have been expanded at a later time to apply more broadly the lessons David learned in these early days. Thus, there are two references to the surrounding nations ("all the nations," v. 5; and "all those nations," v. 8) and one reference to "the ends of the earth" (v. 13).[2] The point seems to be that just as God protected and delivered David when he was surrounded by the hostile forces of King Saul, so also will God protect and deliver his elect people from whatever enemies may surround them.

☙ **Psalm 59** ❧

David may have added these words later himself, or a later writer may have added them to David's earlier psalm to apply it to this broader context.

Marvin E. Tate observes rightly that "the psalm reminds us that we have not escaped the problem of enemies and their evil work in human society. The 'dogs' prowl about in our communities and towns as they did in the ancient world—'dogs' which embody the devouring, malignant persons and forces in human affairs. . . . Law no longer mediated justice."

He reminds us, "Like ancient Israelite communities, we too are dependent on Yahweh for deliverance."[3]

As far as its outline goes, this is another psalm that is divided into two parts by a refrain, like Psalm 57. But here the two parts are also much like one another, even containing repetitions. The simplest outline goes like this: (1) David's appeal to God (vv. 1–5), (2) a description of David's fierce foes (vv. 6–8), (3) a refrain (v. 9), (4) David's second appeal to God (vv. 10–13), (5) a second description of his foes (vv. 14–16), (6) the refrain repeated (v. 17).

David's First Appeal to God

From where we sit, in safety and comfort and frequently surrounded by luxuries, the psalms sometimes seem to be little more than quaint poetry containing noble thoughts. We lose a feel for their urgency. Yet the psalms are often very urgent and their prayers almost desperate. We catch something of the urgent quality of this psalm in the imperatives that begin each of the four swift sentence prayers of verses 1 and 2: "deliver," "protect," "deliver," and "save." These are not casual utterances. In them we can sense David's awareness of danger and of his desperate aloneness except for God.

∽ **Psalm 59** ∾

There is a lesson here, however. The urgency that leads us to utter swift sentence prayers does not preclude our praying thoughtfully and thus presenting a reasoned case to God. I say this because of the second stanza according to the New International Version text. It contains three reasons why God should hear David's prayer.

1. *The danger facing David (v. 3).* God is omniscient. He sees and knows all things. But this does not stop David from calling God's attention to the danger he is facing. "See how they lie in wait for me!" he tells God. "Fierce men conspire against me."

Are you in danger? Tell God about it. Are you discouraged? It is not wrong to call it to God's attention. If you lack wisdom, ask him for wisdom, for he has promised to supply it. David's reminding God of his dangerous situation reminds us of the aged saint who, when people were threatening him, told God, "God, your property is in danger." He knew that he belonged to God, that God saw the problem, loved him, and was able to take care of him. If you are wise, you should let your knowledge of God and his nature draw you to him in prayer rather than turn you away. It is never wrong to honestly tell God anything.

2. *David's innocence (vv. 3–4).* In the last phrase of verse 3 and in verse 4 David protests his innocence: "for no offense or sin of mine, O LORD" and "I have done no wrong." David is not claiming to be sinless, of course. This is not a matter of his innocence before God but rather of his innocence before Saul, his enemy. It is an important point. If you are innocent of wrongdoing before other people, then you can appeal to God bravely and with confidence. If you are guilty of wrongdoing, then you cannot pray boldly and you will appear before God convicted of sin rather than vindicated and assured. Are you innocent before other people? Can you truly say, "I have done no wrong" (v. 4)?

3. *The character of God (v. 5).* One of the most striking features of this psalm is its names for God, and here they appear in profusion: "O Lᴏʀᴅ God Almighty, the God of Israel." In Hebrew this is quite a mouthful of names: *"Yahweh,"* the great personal name of God revealed to Moses on Sinai, meaning "I am who I am"; *"Elohim Sabaoth,"* the God of hosts, with hosts referring both to the armies of Israel and to the heavenly hosts who stand behind them and give victory; *"Elohi Israel,"* the God of Israel, the God who has entered into a lasting covenant relationship with his people. H. C. Leupold says, "The writer recalls God's unique power by employing the various most familiar names by which he was known in Israel."[4] When you can pray, "Lord God, Lord of hosts, God of Israel, my God," you have said a great deal and have a powerful argument.

David's Doglike Foes

Most people who live in the West today have little appreciation for the role of the numerous wild dogs of an ancient Eastern city. For us, dogs are usually pets—or at least guard dogs that patrol an area but are not allowed to roam wild. It was not like that in the East. Occasionally people may have had small dogs as pets. Jesus' words to the Canaanite woman seem to imply this: "It is not right to take the children's bread and toss it to their dogs" (Matt. 15:26). But generally the dogs of an Eastern city were wild scavengers that roamed in packs, particularly at night when they searched the streets and alleys for garbage or other food that may have been discarded by the citizens.

One nineteenth-century writer describes what it was like during a visit he made to Constantinople: "The whole city rang with one vast riot. . . . The yelping, howling, barking, growling, and snarling were all merged into one uniform and continuous even sound, as the noise of frogs becomes when heard at a distance. For hours there was no lull. I went to sleep and woke again, and still, with my windows open, I heard the same tumult going on; nor was it until daybreak that anything like tranquility was restored."[5]

I imagine as I read this that, having lived in a major Western city for twenty-seven years, I would probably not have found the noise of the dogs as overwhelming as that. This Englishman was probably raised in an English village or on the downs. Still, it gives us an idea of what such packs of dogs were like and of how aptly David applies the image to the soldiers who were prowling about his village seeking to kill him.

Should he be afraid of these "dogs"? Hardly, since the Lord his God was laughing at them. These vile creatures are no threat to God; and if they are no threat to God, they are no threat to the one protected by him. The idea of God laughing at his foes takes us back to Psalm 2:4 ("The One enthroned in heaven laughs; the Lord scoffs at them") and Psalm 37:13 ("The Lord laughs at the wicked, for he knows their day is coming").

The Refrain

I will consider the refrain more fully the second time around, when it reappears in verse 17, but I want to note here the one difference in the two versions. Verses 9 and 17 are the same except for the phrase "I watch for you" in the earlier verse, which becomes "I sing praise to you" in the later one. Verse 9 says, "O my Strength, I watch for you; you, O God, are my fortress, my loving God."

"I will watch" reminds us of the minor prophet Habakkuk's similar words when he was in danger and overcome by fear. He declared:

> I will stand at my watch
> and station myself on the ramparts;
> I will look to see what he will say to me,
> and what answer I am to give to this complaint.
>
> Habakkuk 2:1

Habakkuk did not understand why the things that were happening in Israel in his day were happening, any more than David understood what the Lord was doing when he allowed him to be hunted by Saul's soldiers. But Habakkuk did the same thing David did. Habakkuk committed himself to God and waited faithfully and expectantly for God's deliverance.

There are many cases in which you and I can do no more. We cannot alter these situations, but we can commit them to God and wait for his solution.

David's Second Appeal to God

In the psalmist's first appeal (vv. 1–5), the emphasis seemed to be on David's danger and therefore on the bloodthirsty men who had been set against him. In this second parallel appeal (vv. 10–13), David's description of the danger shifts to what he is asking God to do to these enemies.

He is asking God to destroy them, of course: "bring them down" (v. 11), "let them be caught in their pride" (v. 12), "consume them in wrath, consume them till they are no more" (v. 13). But what is unique in this second appeal is his asking that these enemies not be destroyed at once but rather gradually so that people will see it, learn from it, and not forget God's justice. David says:

> But do not kill them, O Lord our shield,
> or my people will forget.
>
> verse 11

This says something important about evil and God's willingness to let evildoers survive for a time. For some this is an offense, even a reason for disbelieving in God: "If there is a God, why would he permit such things to happen?" But here is one answer: God allows evil to flourish for a time so that we might learn from it. We can see that evil is short-lived. We can learn that sin carries the seeds of its own destruction in itself. We can know that judgment does come upon the wicked in the end. If God did not permit evil, we would not learn any of this and would not grow spiritually.

Verse 13 sums this up. When evil emerges, is tolerated for a time, is allowed to stagnate and fall because of its own inner corruption, and then is eventually judged decisively by God, "Then it will be known to the ends of the earth that God rules over Jacob" (v. 13). This understanding of evil must have been in David's mind for a long time, for these are almost the same words he used when he went out to fight Goliath. He told the Philistine champion, "This day the LORD will hand you over to me, and I'll strike you down and cut off your head . . . and the whole world will know that there is a God in Israel" (1 Sam. 17:46).

David's Foes and God Almighty

The fifth section of the psalm is like the second, even repeating phrases, but there is this difference: In section two David was describing the conduct of his enemies, portraying them as wild dogs. Here he is noting their punishment, particularly their howls of frustration when they are "not satisfied."

Remember that. Not only does evil carry within it the seeds of its own destruction, but also it is not capable of being satisfied. In fact, it is the very nature of evil to be dissatisfied: wanting, but never having enough; eating, but never getting full;

grasping, but always seeing the object of the desire slipping from its hands. There is a picture of this in God's judgment on the serpent in the Garden of Eden, described in Genesis 3. God told the serpent, "You will crawl on your belly and you will eat dust all the days of your life" (v. 14). A snake does not eat dirt, of course. This is a way of saying that for those who pursue evil everything they taste will turn to ashes in their mouths.

As for the godly, they know that God will "prepare a table" for them even "in the presence of [their] enemies" and that "goodness and love will follow [them]" all the days of their lives (Ps. 23:5–6).

The Refrain

Now we come to the second occurrence of the refrain. It is a great testimony, of course ("O my Strength, I sing praise to you; you, O God, are my fortress, my loving God"), particularly when we remember that outwardly the psalmist's situation had not changed a bit. The same circumstances that caused David to cry out to God in verses 1 and 2 are still there. But here at the very end he is not only testifying that God is his "strength" and "fortress," he is actually singing praises to God in the very midst of his danger. In fact, the singing begins even a verse before this, in verse 16.

What has brought him to this point of vigorous jubilation? The answer is in the slight variation between verses 9 and 17. In verse 9 he is waiting on God, watching for his eventual deliverance. It is because he has been waiting and because God has provided encouragement, though not yet the expected deliverance, that David can sing. In Hebrew the words *watch* and *sing* are identical except for one letter, which is a way of saying, I suppose, that keeping one's eyes on God is only a stroke away from singing his praises and otherwise rejoicing in him.

◌◌ **Psalm 59** ◌◌

Do you lack joy? Is it hard for you to sing God's praises? If so, it is probably because you are not watching for God, are not looking to him. Remember Habakkuk, whom I referred to earlier as one who was waiting on his watchtower to see what God would say to him. Nothing changed outwardly for Habakkuk, either. He was as much in danger and as much perplexed at the end of his prophecy as at the beginning. But Habakkuk was changed as a result of waiting upon God, and for that reason his short book ends in what we can only regard as singing:

> Though the fig tree does not bud
>   and there are no grapes on the vines,
> though the olive crop fails
>   and the fields produce no food,
> though there are no sheep in the pen
>   and no cattle in the stalls,
> yet I will rejoice in the LORD,
>   I will be joyful in God my Savior.
>
> The Sovereign LORD is my strength;
>   he makes my feet like the feet of a deer,
>   he enables me to go on the heights.
>   Habakkuk 3:17–19

Those are the words of one who has learned to wait on God and trust him. They are words any Christian should be able to echo.

Alexander MacLaren says, "Trust [God] as what he is, and trust him because of what he is, and see to it that your faith lays hold on the living God himself and on nothing besides."[6] If you do that, regardless of the circumstances that surround you, even if you are surrounded by "dogs" who seek your life, you will end up singing.

Psalm 60

You have rejected us, O God, and burst forth
      upon us;
  you have been angry—now restore us!
You have shaken the land and torn it open;
  mend its fractures, for it is quaking.
You have shown your people desperate times;
  you have given us wine that makes us stagger.

But for those who fear you, you have raised a
      banner
  to be unfurled against the bow.   *Selah*

Save us and help us with your right hand,
  that those you love may be delivered.
God has spoken from his sanctuary:
  "In triumph I will parcel out Shechem
  and measure off the Valley of Succoth.
Gilead is mine, and Manasseh is mine;
  Ephraim is my helmet,
  Judah my scepter.
Moab is my washbasin,
  upon Edom I toss my sandal;
  over Philistia I shout in triumph."

Who will bring me to the fortified city?
  Who will lead me to Edom?
Is it not you, O God, who have rejected us
  and no longer go out with our armies?

Give us aid against the enemy,
    for the help of man is worthless.
With God we will gain the victory,
    and he will trample down our enemies.

If God Does Not Go with Us

One of the things you and I do when we fall into sin or disobedience is try to get away from God, like Jonah when he rejected God's call to go as a missionary preacher to Nineveh and instead ran away to Tarshish. We think that if we can get away from God we can do as we like. Jonah got on a boat sailing in the exact opposite direction and thought he was doing quite well until God pursued him by sending a storm that eventually caused the sailors to throw him overboard, hoping that this would get the storm to stop. Jonah was swallowed by a great fish, and the only time he really felt that he had gotten away from God was when he was in the stomach of the fish, believed that he was going to die there, and concluded that God had abandoned him. And then he didn't like it.

The worst thing in all of life is to be abandoned by God, and after this life hell is the final abandonment by God. The only wise course for anyone is to seek the presence of God always and in all places and to say, as David seems to say in Psalm 60, "If God does not go with me, I will not go."

The Historical Background

Psalm 60 is the next to last of the psalms with an explicit historical setting from the life of David. The last is Psalm 63.

The setting of the psalm is given in the title, and the title is the longest such introductory title in the Psalter. It occupies three and a half lines in our text and about the same amount of space in the standard Hebrew Bible. In the Hebrew Bible the titles are numbered along with the verses, and the title of this psalm is actually its first two verses.

It tells us that these words are about the time David "fought Aram Naharaim and Aram Zobah [that is, the Arameans of the Mesopotamian River valley],[1] and when Joab returned and struck down twelve thousand Edomites in the Valley of Salt." The only possible time for these battles is after David had become king and had reigned for a considerable number of years. But if this is so, then Psalm 60 is an important historical document, for, as Derek Kidner says, "[Except] for this psalm and its title we should have no inkling of the resilience of David's hostile neighbors at the peak of his power."[2] He means that the only other accounts we have of this period speak of it as a time of uninterrupted military victories.

This suggests two strange things about Psalm 60. First, the title is about a victory—Joab's victory over the Edomites in the Valley of Salt—but the psalm is about a defeat ("You have rejected us, O God, and burst forth upon us," v. 1). Second, as I have indicated and so far as we can tell, the title sets the psalm in a soaring account of David's many and geographically widespread victories. Why should it introduce a defeat by such a context?

But maybe that is the lesson. Let me explain.

The background is in 2 Samuel 8:1–14.[3] Several things are recorded in the part of the book immediately before this. First, David becomes king over all Israel (2 Sam. 5:1–5). Second, he conquers Jerusalem and makes it his capital (5:6–16). Third, he achieves decisive victories over the Philistines (5:17–25). Fourth, he brings the ark to Jerusalem as a focus for the people's worship (ch. 6). Fifth, God sends Nathan to him with the greatest message David received in his entire lifetime, that God was going to establish his throne forever (ch. 7). It was a prophecy of the Messiah, which David immediately recognized. These are the unprecedented events preceding chapter 8, and it is immediately after them that the chapter about David's many military victories, the setting for Psalm 60, occurs.

Here are the highlights of this chapter:

> In the course of time, David defeated the Philistines and subdued them, and he took Metheg Ammah from the control of the Philistines.
>
> David also defeated the Moabites. . . .
>
> Moreover, David fought Hadadezer, son of Rehob, king of Zobah, when he went to restore his control along the Euphrates River. [These are the areas mentioned in the title of Psalm 60.] David captured a thousand of his chariots, seven thousand charioteers and twenty thousand foot soldiers. He hamstrung all but a hundred of the chariot horses.
>
> When the Arameans of Damascus came to help Hadadezer king of Zobah, David struck down twenty-two thousand of them. He put garrisons in the Aramean kingdom of Damascus, and the Arameans became subject to him and brought tribute. The LORD gave David victory everywhere he went. . . .
>
> And David became famous after he returned from striking down eighteen thousand Edomites in the Valley of Salt.
>
> He put garrisons throughout Edom, and all the Edomites became subject to David. The LORD gave David victory wherever he went.
>
> 2 Samuel 8:1–6, 13–14

What seems to have happened, if we put the title of Psalm 60 together with this account, is that the Edomites took advantage of David's being away from Jerusalem, fighting along the

Psalm 60

Euphrates River, and staged an uprising. They must have suc-
ceeded in this to the extent described in Psalm 60, as a result
of which David dispatched Joab, one of his chief commanders, to subdue the Edomites. Joab did this, achieving the victory described in the title of Psalm 60, after which David
returned and completed the conquest, even of the Edomite
strongholds. That sequence of events might explain why Joab
is credited with killing twelve thousand Edomites in Psalm 60,
while David is credited with striking down eighteen thousand
Edomites in 2 Samuel 8:13.[4]

This tells us that even in times of unprecedented blessing
there are nevertheless defeats. Some Jewish cities were still
being overrun by enemies. Some people were still being killed.
So then, should we expect things to be different? It is a fallen
world. Even in times of blessing we can expect some things to
go wrong. In fact, even when we are closest to the Lord ourselves, we can be sure that there are still areas of our lives that
will cause us trouble and need correcting.

As far as an outline goes, the psalm seems to fall into three
parts of four verses each: (1) a lament on the occasion of a
great defeat (vv. 1–4), (2) an appeal to God and God's answer,
an oracle (vv. 5–8), and (3) two important lessons to be drawn
(vv. 9–12).

Defeat in the Midst of Victory

We do not know specifics of the defeat that came to Israel
at this time, but the opening verses of Psalm 60 portray it as
a great disaster. It was so great that two powerful images are
used to describe what it was like.

First, an earthquake (v. 2). We know how damaging and ter-
rifying earthquakes can be because we have heard accounts of
many of them: a recent earthquake in San Francisco, the earth-

quake that killed many people in Japan, earthquakes in Central
America, Turkey, and the former Soviet Union, to mention just
a few. In these earthquakes tremendous damage was done and
many lost their lives. It is easy to see how such a strong image
might apply to a military defeat in which city walls have been
broken down and some of the defenders killed. David says, "You
have shaken the land and torn it open; mend its fractures, for
it is quaking" (v. 2).

The second image describes the effect of the battle and
defeat on the people. It is the image of drunkenness: "You
have shown your people desperate times; you have given us
wine that makes us stagger" (v. 3). This is a frequent Old Testament image for God's outpoured wrath, being found not
only in the psalms but also in the prophets. The image occurs
in Psalm 75:8:

> In the hand of the LORD is a cup
>   full of foaming wine mixed with spices;
> he pours it out, and all the wicked of the earth
>   drink it down to its very dregs.

This image is also in Isaiah 51:17, 22; Jeremiah 13:13;
25:15–16; 49:12; and other passages. Isaiah 51:17, a typical
passage, says:

> Awake, awake!
>   Rise up, O Jerusalem,
> you who have drunk from the hand of the LORD
>   the cup of his wrath,
> you who have drained to its dregs
>   the goblet that makes men stagger.

We might say that the attack by the Edomites left the people
reeling from the blow.

∽ Psalm 60 ∽

Yet the worst thing about this defeat, as David describes it, is that it was because the Lord was angry with the people and had rejected them (v. 1). This does not seem to refer to everyone. For example, there is no reason to think that God was angry with David, at least in this period of his life. Nor was he even angry with all the people in the defeated territories. In fact, the fourth verse makes a distinction, saying, "But for those who fear you, you have raised a banner to be unfurled against the bow." These people were obedient and godly. Still, there were some who had displeased God, and David takes their acts and God's consequent displeasure seriously. Because of their sin many were defeated, just as the entire armies of Israel were defeated at Ai because of Achan's disobedience at Jericho (cf. Joshua 7).

Charles Spurgeon made an interesting comment on this point. He said, "To be cast off by God is the worst calamity that can befall a man or a people; but the worst form of it is when the person is not aware of it and is indifferent to it."[5] David was aware of it, however, and he wrote this psalm to show that he was not indifferent.

Let's apply this to the church. Isn't it true that the church fails to achieve great victories because of the sin of some? Churches are sometimes torn open because of a few factious members. Denominations fail to achieve their potential because some bring disgrace on the gospel or others deny or even attack it. What shall we do when we see that happening? We need to make sure we are not the cause of the trouble, first of all. But then we need to do something else too. We need to rally around the banner God has given us, and that banner is the gospel. Those who fear the Lord will do that (v. 4). Their actions will show that they fear him, and he will provide for them and defend them.

ᐯ **Psalm 60** ᐸ

It is significant that a *selah* occurs at this point in the psalm. It probably means "stop and consider, pay attention to that."

An Appeal to God and God's Answer

The second section of the psalm contains an appeal to God to help those who have been attacked by the Edomites (v. 5), followed by God's answer in the form of an oracle (vv. 6–8). The oracle follows so closely upon the appeal that we know that faith has already won a victory.

There are two ways verses 6 through 8 may be understood. They are introduced as a word that "God has spoken from his sanctuary." So it is possible, first, that this was a special revelation from God that could have been brought to David by Nathan or one of the other priests or prophets. In that case, it is a statement that God has given the land of Israel to the Jewish people and a promise that he would give them victory over the enemies that were trying to take it from them. If this is that kind of oracle, it may have been preserved in writing separately from the psalm, which might explain why verses 5 through 12 also appear as the latter half of Psalm 108, verses 6 to 13.[6]

The other way of looking at these verses is suggested by the fact that the place names are not what we might expect at this point in David's career—we would expect the names of the tribal territories perhaps—and by the fact that they seem to come from and trace the early history of the occupation of the land from the time of the patriarch Jacob onward. Shechem was the place Jacob settled after his return to Canaan from Paddan Aram, where he had lived for twenty years with his uncle and later father-in-law, Laban (Gen. 33:18). Succoth was the last place he had been prior to that (Gen. 33:17). These two places represent the eastern and western sides of the Jordan River. Gilead and Manasseh represent larger areas of the eastern side of the Jordan River occupied by Israel at the time of the conquest under Joshua. Ephraim and Judah represent the most prominent tribes to the west.[7] If these names are meant to remind us of this early history and of the fact that God had given the land to the people from the time of the patriarchs, then verses 6 through 9 are not necessarily an oracle from David's own time but rather a new phrasing of these older promises.

But notice this: In either case, as H. C. Leupold writes, "The word of God (vv. 6–8) is made the basis of [the faith expressed in verse 5]. Thus faith should always seek the foundation of the Word of God."[8]

Biblical faith is not optimism, as some think. Nor is it a positive mental attitude worked up to help us through tough times. According to the Bible, faith is believing the Word of God and acting on it, which is what David expresses in this psalm and what he apparently did in actuality. That is, because God had promised him victory over Edom, as well as over Moab and Philistia, David sent Joab to fight the armies of Edom in the Valley of Salt.

Wouldn't we be more active in gospel work if we believed God's promise to bless the preaching of the gospel? God has said that he will never allow his Word to return to him empty (Isa. 55:10–11). Some believed that and have won nearly whole cities, even continents to Christ. David Livingstone believed it and won Africa.

Two Lessons

Precisely when was Psalm 60 written? We know from 2 Samuel 8 that David eventually joined Joab and conquered Edom, placing garrisons throughout the country. In the last stanza of this psalm he is thinking about that final triumph, asking, "Who will bring me to the fortified city? Who will lead me to Edom?" (v. 9). It would seem, therefore, that David wrote the psalm while on his campaign near the Euphrates River after Joab was dispatched but before the final victories. What is in David's mind at this time? What lessons was he learning as he reflected, first on the defeat of the people by Edom and second on the promises of God to give an eventual victory? It seems to me that there were two of them.

1. *Only God can give victory.* There were a number of well-fortified cities in Edom, the source of the country's strength and great pride. But when David speaks of "*the* fortified city" he can only mean Petra, the most inaccessible and apparently impregnable mountain stronghold of Edom. I had the privilege of visiting Petra many years ago. It is approached through a narrow cut in the limestone cliffs that winds inward for about two miles and is called a *siq*. The cliffs rise upward for thousands of feet on both sides, and in places the passage is so narrow that no more than two horses can pass abreast. A handful of brave men could defend this *siq* against an army. But even if the passage could be breached, the defenders could retreat into the mountains surrounding the hidden inner valley and defend themselves from there. Only God could give victory over a fortress like that, and David knew it. So David cried to God, acknowledging that "the help of man is worthless" (v. 11).

2. *We must ask for it.* That is the second lesson David was learning from this defeat and God's promise. He was learning that although only God can give victory, we must nevertheless ask for it. And so he did. That is what he is doing in the final stanza of the psalm. Moreover, because he is asking for help he anticipates God's positive answer, saying:

◌ Psalm 60 ◌

With God we will gain the victory,
    and he will trample down our enemies.

                             verse 12

Thus, as Leupold says, "The psalm closes on a strong note of confidence which was engendered by the promises of God, which were grasped in faith."[9]

You and I are not kings, as David was. We do not have military battles to fight. We have never seen an Edomite. But I want to suggest that the lessons of this psalm are directly applicable to us in terms of the spiritual battles we are called to fight. We are members of the kingdom of the Lord Jesus Christ, and our task is to advance his kingdom in this spiritually hostile world. The apostle Paul said, "For our struggle is not against flesh and blood, but against the rulers, against the authorities, against the powers of this dark world and against the spiritual forces of evil in the heavenly realms" (Eph. 6:12). Compared to the conquest of these hostile spiritual forces, the victory over Edom and the overthrow of its mountain stronghold Petra was a piece of cake. How can we gain this greater victory? Not by ourselves, or even with the help of other Christians. In this battle "the help of man is [truly] worthless." We need God to fight with us and on our behalf.

The second lesson applies to us too: We must ask for God's help. The Book of James says, "You do not have, because you do not ask God" (James 4:2). Jesus said, "Ask and it will be given to you; seek and you will find; knock and the door will be opened to you" (Matt. 7:7). We can ask for many things wrongly and so fail to receive them. James speaks of that too (4:3). But the one thing we can be sure of receiving is victory on behalf of the gospel. Nebuchadnezzar had a vision that he could not remember but that troubled him greatly. It was a vision of a great statue representing in sequence all the many great kingdoms of this world. At the end of the vision a rock not cut by human hands struck the statue and destroyed it, and then grew up to become "a huge mountain" that "filled the whole earth" (Dan. 2:34–35). That rock is the Lord Jesus Christ, and that mountain is his kingdom, which is destined to triumph.

If you believe that, then this is the banner around which you must rally and on behalf of which you can confidently fight.

Psalm 60

Psalm 61

Hear my cry, O God;
   listen to my prayer.

From the ends of the earth I call to you,
   I call as my heart grows faint;
    lead me to the rock that is higher than I.
For you have been my refuge,
   a strong tower against the foe.

I long to dwell in your tent forever
   and take refuge in the shelter of your wings.   *Selah*
For you have heard my vows, O God;
   you have given me the heritage of those who
       fear your name.

Increase the days of the king's life,
   his years for many generations.
May he be enthroned in God's presence forever;
   appoint your love and faithfulness to protect him.

Then will I ever sing praise to your name
   and fulfill my vows day after day.

The Rock That Is Higher Than I

*O*n the *Trinity Hymnal,* the hymn-book we use in our church, William O. Cushing's hymn "O Safe to the Rock That Is Higher Than I" is linked to Psalm 94 because of verse 22, which speaks of God as a rock of refuge. But it is hard to read Psalm 61 without supposing that Cushing had it in mind rather than Psalm 94 when he composed the hymn. Psalm 61 says, "Lead me to the rock that is higher than I," and Cushing wrote:

O safe to the Rock that is higher than I
My soul in its conflicts and sorrows would fly;
So sinful, so weary, thine, thine would I be;
Thou blest Rock of Ages, I'm hiding in thee.
Hiding in thee, hiding in thee—
Thou blest Rock of Ages, I'm hiding in thee.

People who have lived with the Lord for any length of time know the force of that hymn and the image it is based upon. Life is filled with sorrows, and there are times in life when there is literally no one else to whom we can turn for understanding, comfort, or help. Some people spend most of their lives alone. Others are surrounded by an unsympathetic family, perhaps those who are not Christians and resent the believer's convictions and lifestyle. You may have an unbelieving husband or wife, or your coworkers may resent you. Or you may simply be old, and all your friends and relatives have died. Whatever the case, many know what it is like to have no one human to whom they can turn for understanding. Yet if they are Christians and have any experience of the Lord at all, they know that God is a rock to which they can turn, a rock higher and wiser and stronger than they are themselves.

The title of Psalm 61 identifies it as a psalm of David, but it could be from nearly any period in his life, since we know that David often felt alone, even after he had become king. There would have been many times in the wilderness, when he was fleeing from Saul, when he would have felt alone. But he would also have felt alone when he had to flee again later, when his son Absalom was trying to kill him and take over the kingdom, and even when he was again secure in Jerusalem but surrounded by counselors, many of whom he could not trust.

There are various ways of outlining this psalm. Some divide it into two parts of four verses each, separated at the *selah* following verse 4.[1] Leupold divides the psalm into three petitions, the first two ending with a reason for the petition, the third with a vow.[2] Alexander Maclaren argues that there is an introductory verse, followed by three matched pairs of verses, ending with an additional single verse to match verse 1.[3] I think all these outlines are valid, but none is more helpful than the others. Psalm 61 is a very simple psalm, and the best way to study it is merely to look at each of the five main points in order.

◌⟋ **Psalm 61** ⟍◌

Trust When Far from Home

The setting for a psalm provides the background for interpreting it, and in this case the psalmist is far from home. He feels he is very far away indeed, because he is calling to God from what he regards as the very "ends of the earth" (v. 2).

For any Jew the center of the universe was (and is) Jerusalem, where the ark of God was located. So the phrase "ends of the earth" must mean that David was far from or felt himself to be far from Jerusalem. Is this to be taken literally, as a geographical reference? If so, it could refer to any time David was absent from the capital—when he was fleeing from Saul or Absalom or when he was away on a military campaign. Verses 6 and 7 make clear that at the time of writing David was already king, so the days when he was fleeing from Saul are eliminated. David could be writing during the days of Absalom's rebellion. Again, the placing of Psalm 61 immediately after Psalm 60 might suggest that the psalm was written at the time of the campaign along the Euphrates River, which is the earlier psalm's setting. Certainly the words "ends of the earth" would be more appropriate to that location than the Judean wilderness where David fled from Absalom. It is very possible that this is the time involved.

But there is another possibility, and that is that the words "ends of the earth" are metaphorical. This idea appeals to Marvin E. Tate, who concludes his study with a section suggesting that the chief value of the psalm is its metaphorical richness. He believes that "the dominant metaphor in the psalm is that of distance from God . . . a sense of far-awayness from the divine presence, an at-the-end-of-the-earth experience" and that the psalm was written to overcome this faraway feeling. He adds, "Breaking down a perceived distance and the creation of a sense of nearness and presence is a major function of prayer."[4]

This may be right, and in any case it is how you and I should apply the words to ourselves, at least in most instances. From time to time, perhaps often, you and I feel far from God. We read the Bible, but it doesn't speak to us as it once did. We pray, but the heavens seem to be made of brass and God does not answer the requests we lay before him. We even feel far from God in church. What should we do when we feel like this? We should not stop reading the Bible, praying, or going to church. We should continue those things. But in addition we should do as David did and learn to pray along the lines of this psalm.

A Rock Higher Than Ourselves

The second point to notice about Psalm 61 is the image David uses for God in verse 2, calling him "the rock that is higher than I." The idea of God being a rock is common in the psalms, appearing twenty times.[5] In fact, it occurs three times in the next psalm, Psalm 62. One of the most well-rounded treatments of the image is in Psalm 18, where it is used four times in an interesting progressive sequence:

> The LORD is my rock (v. 2).
> My God is my rock (v. 2).
> Who is the Rock except our God? (v. 31).
> Praise be to my Rock! (v. 46).

The thought of God being a rock is prominent in the Davidic psalms because David had used the rocks of the Judean wilderness as places of refuge and protection during the years he was forced to hide from King Saul and Absalom. David knew every cranny, track, and hiding place in the vast rocky wilderness.

So when he fled to the rocks he knew that he was safe in their protection.

Each of the psalms has its own way of portraying God as a rock. There are two unique features to David's use of the rock image in Psalm 61.

1. *This rock is "higher" than David.* It is natural to think of God being higher or greater than ourselves when we are suffering some severe reversal of fortune, when we are somehow down and out. We know we need God then. But when we are on top, as David seems to have been at this time—he was the king of all Israel, after all—we forget about God and consider ourselves able to deal with anything. David never made this mistake. He never forgot that God was infinitely above him and that it was always God he needed. The people of Israel may have looked to David as their rock, but David looked to a rock that was higher than he. He knew he was no stronger than the rock that overshadowed him and on which he could stand firmly.

2. *We must be led to this rock.* The other unique feature of David's speaking of God as his rock in Psalm 61 is that he asks to be "led" to it—that is, led to God. It is hard to know exactly what David was thinking of when he wrote this, but Charles Haddon Spurgeon, the great Baptist preacher, pointed out that, for our part, not only do we need a rock, we also need the Holy Spirit to lead us to him. Our rock is Christ, but none of us come to Christ by ourselves. We need the Holy Spirit to quicken our dead souls, awaken us to our spiritual need, renew our wills, and bring us to the point of personal commitment to the Savior.

In Spurgeon's day mariners were often drowned when their ships ran upon the rocks of the rocky coast of England and the men were cast into the water. At times they would find themselves struggling at the base of high cliffs and knew they would be safe if they could only get up the steep slippery face of the rocks. But they could not. At one place, according to Spurgeon, a man who lived at the top of one of these cliffs carved stone steps into the rock face so wrecked mariners could climb up. And when the steps became badly worn and impassable over time, someone else added stanchions and a chain railing to help the struggling survivors.

Observed Spurgeon, "How infinitely higher than we are is the salvation of God. We are low and grovelling, but it towers like some tall cliff far above us. This is its glory, and it is our delight when we have once climbed [onto] the rock and claimed an interest in it; but while we are as yet trembling seekers, the glory and sublimity of salvation appall us, and we feel that we are too unworthy even to be partakers of it; hence we are led to cry for grace upon grace, and to see how dependent we are for everything, not only for the Savior, but for the power to believe on him."[6] Our salvation from beginning to end is of God and is due entirely to grace.

Is God your rock? Have you been led to him? If you have not trusted in Jesus Christ yet, there is nothing wrong with asking God to lead you to him. It is a case of saying, "I do believe; help me overcome my unbelief!" (Mark 9:24). It is a case of acknowledging your utter need of God's grace. If you pray that, you will find that it is a prayer God clearly loves to answer.

What God Is to His Trusting People

The next thing to notice about Psalm 61 is that its second stanza adds to the image of God as David's rock by four metaphors that elaborate what God is to his trusting people. God is so great that any number of images might be provided at this point. What is significant about these four is that they are arranged to become increasingly warm and intimate.

1. *A refuge.* This image is closest to that of God being a rock and, in fact, is frequently linked to it: "my rock, in whom I take refuge" (Ps. 18:2), "my rock of refuge" (Ps. 31:2; 71:3), "my mighty rock, my refuge" (Ps. 62:7), and "the rock in whom I take refuge" (Ps. 94:22). It calls to mind a retreat such as David used when fleeing from King Saul, for it was in the rocks of the Judean wilderness that David found his refuge.

2. *A strong tower.* A tower is a refuge for people in times of attack from enemies, but it differs from a wilderness refuge in that it is part of a walled city. Therefore, the idea here is not of a person fleeing from home but of someone defending himself at home when threatened by hostile forces. Presumably he is not alone in this condition. Others would be taking refuge in the tower with him and would be helping him defend it.

3. *A tent.* A tent conjures up a domestic scene in which a host might welcome strangers, as Abraham welcomed the three heavenly visitors outside his tent near the great trees of Mamre. Such a visitor would be entitled to his host's most solicitous care and protection. Yet there may be more in the image than this, since the word *tent* is also translated as tabernacle, and in the Old Testament it frequently refers to the tabernacle where the ark of God was kept. If David is using the word in this sense, then he is asking to dwell where God himself dwells, an idea he also expresses elsewhere:[7]

> One thing I ask of the LORD,
>   this is what I seek:
> that I may dwell in the house of the LORD
>   all the days of my life,
> to gaze upon the beauty of the LORD
>   and to seek him in his temple.
>   Psalm 27:4

Psalm 61

This means that the images used thus far move us from the wilderness to the fortified city, presumably Jerusalem, to the tabernacle area, which means closer and closer to God.

4. *A sheltering mother bird.* Thus we are prepared for the last and most intimate image of all, that of dwelling under the shadow of God's wings. When we studied Psalm 57 we saw that commentators often interpret this image as having to do with the wings of the cherubim on the lid of the ark of God within the tabernacle, which would make a natural sequence in this stanza, especially if the tent image refers to the tabernacle where the ark was kept. But I argued in the earlier study that, strictly speaking, the wings are not called the wings of the cherubim but the wings of God, and that this is an even more powerful and intimate image. Some might think it indelicate, but David would not consider it wrong to want to be sheltered beneath the wings and against the very breast of God.

Nor should we. Never fear to be intimate with God. God desires to be intimate with you and is only hurt when you remain at a distance or draw back from his embrace. You have to learn what intimacy with God means; but if and as you do, you will find that God will be far more intimate with you than you have ever imagined he could be.

A Prayer Fulfilled in the Messiah

Verses 6 and 7 switch from the first to the third person, the writer apparently ceasing to pray for himself and pray instead that God will "increase the days of the king's life, his years for many generations," that he will be "enthroned in God's presence forever" and that God will appoint his "love and faithfulness to protect him." Many commentators believe that another hand added these words, perhaps at a later date. However, it can also be argued that David is writing about himself as king, merely switching to the third person from the first for stylistic effect. The last verse seems to imply this since it returns to the first person, promising that the speaker will praise God if the earlier petition is answered. David could do that if God prolonged his reign for generations.

Yet this must also be said: Whether this prayer was by David or is for David, ultimately it is about and is fulfilled in the Messiah. "Increase the days of the king's life"? That can easily be understood of an earthly king. "His years for many generations"? That too perhaps, by stretching things a little. But not, "May he be enthroned in God's presence *forever*," at least not if that is understood literally.

And it probably should be.

I say that because this is the way David responded when God sent Nathan to him to promise that a descendant of his would sit upon his throne forever:

> When your days are over and you rest with your fathers, I will raise up your offspring to succeed you, who will come from your own body, and I will establish his kingdom. He is the one who will build a house for my Name, and I will establish the throne of his kingdom forever.
>
> 2 Samuel 7:12–13

Some of that might be understood as having been fulfilled in Solomon, David's immediate successor. But not the forever part, which David seems to have recognized since he responded, "Is this your usual way of dealing with man, O Sovereign LORD?" (v. 19). Nothing merely of man lasts forever. So if God was promising a forever kingdom, it must be a kingdom to be established and maintained by a divine Messiah, who is God become man. The promise made to David was about the eternal kingdom of the Lord Jesus Christ, and if this is what David was thinking about in Psalm 61, the psalm is another of the Messianic psalms.

∽ **Psalm 61** ∽

Enduring Praise for God

As we look back over Psalm 61 we are reminded that David began it feeling at "the ends of the earth," thus, far from God. But as he thought about God and prayed to him he drew closer to God and grew in confidence until he ends actually expecting to be established in Jerusalem, his capital, for many days and many generations. That is something to praise God for. And that, quite naturally, is how the psalm ends:

> Then will I ever sing praise to your name
> and fulfill my vows day after day.
>
> verse 8

Shouldn't that be true for you as well? It is not only David who had such a great God, or those who lived with him in this Old Testament period. His God is our God, and it is our privilege to know him even more intimately than David did, for we know him in the Lord Jesus Christ. Jesus is the rock that is higher than we are, infinitely higher. He is very God of very God, as the creeds say. He is the Rock of Ages. But he is also the rock that has been cleft for us, crucified, that we might be saved from sin:

> Rock of Ages, cleft for me,
> Let me hide myself in Thee.

Jesus is our refuge, but not only a refuge from human enemies and foes. He is a refuge from the wrath of God to be poured out at the final judgment. He is our tower that we can run into and be safe. He is our tabernacle. The apostle John used this very word when he wrote, "The Word became flesh and made his dwelling among us" (John 1:14). In the Greek the words "made his dwelling among us" literally mean tabernacled. He is also the one who said of the city of Jerusalem,

"O Jerusalem, Jerusalem, you who kill the prophets and stone those sent to you, how often I have longed to gather your children together, as a hen gathers her chicks under her wings, but you were not willing" (Matt. 23:37). But he has gathered *us* to himself.

Sometimes we need to feel we are at "the ends of the earth" before we can discover how wonderful Jesus is. That is what Augustine was thinking of when he wrote, "They that are godly are oppressed and vexed in the church or congregation for this purpose: that when they are pressed, they should cry; and when they cry, that they should be heard; and when they are heard, that they should laud and praise God."[8] We will be happy Christians if we learn to do just that.

Psalm 61

Psalm 62

My soul finds rest in God alone;
    my salvation comes from him.
He alone is my rock and my salvation;
    he is my fortress, I will never be shaken.

How long will you assault a man?
    Would all of you throw him down—
    this leaning wall, this tottering fence?
They fully intend to topple him
    from his lofty place;
    they take delight in lies.
With their mouths they bless,
    but in their hearts they curse.   *Selah*

Find rest, O my soul, in God alone;
    my hope comes from him.
He alone is my rock and my salvation;
    he is my fortress, I will not be shaken.
My salvation and my honor depend on God;
    he is my mighty rock, my refuge.
Trust in him at all times, O people;
    pour out your hearts to him,
    for God is our refuge.   *Selah*

Lowborn men are but a breath,
    the highborn are but a lie;
if weighed on a balance, they are nothing;
    together they are only a breath.

Do not trust in extortion
  or take pride in stolen goods;
though your riches increase,
  do not set your heart on them.

One thing God has spoken,
  two things have I heard:
that you, O God, are strong,
  and that you, O Lord, are loving.
Surely you will reward each person
  according to what he has done.

Rest in God Alone

Do you ever feel like an endangered species? If we are to believe what we read in the papers, there are a lot of endangered species these days, and many powerful organizations have come into existence to try to save them. There are endangered whales, endangered seals, endangered plants, even the endangered snail darter that held up a major hydroelectric project in the South for many years. When we are discouraged, depressed, or threatened we sometimes feel that we too are one of these endangered species and that we are soon going to be destroyed, wiped out, and forgotten.

David felt this way. That is what Psalm 62 is all about. He was surrounded by enemies who were treating him as if he were a leaning, tottering wall, and they were doing everything they could to knock him down. Yet in spite of their hostility, in this psalm David is not worrying about them but rather is trusting God. He calls God his rock and his fortress and says, "I will never be shaken" (v. 2).

That is probably the most important thing to be said about this psalm. David is in danger, but in spite of the danger his trust in God is so strong that the psalm is wonderfully serene and confident. In fact, it is utterly confident. Many people have noticed this. H. C. Leupold wrote, "There is scarcely another psalm that reveals such an absolute and undisturbed peace, in which confidence in God is so completely unshaken, and in which assurance is so strong that not even one single petition is voiced throughout the psalm."[1] J. J. Stewart Perowne observed, "Scarcely anywhere do we find faith in God more nobly asserted, more victoriously triumphant; the vanity of man, of human strength and riches, more clearly confessed; courage in the midst of peril more calm and more unshaken, than in this psalm."[2]

Clearly this is a psalm for you if you feel threatened or in danger.

The psalm falls naturally into three stanzas of four verses each, the three parts separated by the *selah*s that follow verses 4 and 8. But the last four verses are longer than the earlier ones, which encouraged the translators of the New International Version to divide the psalm into four parts. In what follows, I am holding to the NIV arrangement.

God and the Psalmist's Enemies

The first stanza (vv. 1–4) introduces us to the three interacting agents in this psalm: God, the psalmist, and the psalmist's enemies. His enemies are trying to throw him down, but David is trusting God, his "rock," his "salvation," and his "fortress" (v. 2). The critical point is that David is trusting in God only, in God alone.

It is hard to see this in the English text, because the Hebrew is almost untranslatable, but in the Hebrew text the word *only* or *alone* occurs five times in the first six verses (vv. 1, 2, 4, 5, 6), and also once more in verse nine. The Hebrew word is *'ak*, and the reason its use in the psalm is almost untranslatable is that no one English word seems to be an adequate translation in all six occurrences. Moreover, in the Hebrew text the word occurs at the beginning of each of the six verses for emphasis, and that too does not lend itself to any easy translation in English. *Alone* is probably the best word for us to use, which is what the New International Version uses in four of the six occurrences: "My soul finds rest in God *alone*" (v. 1), "He *alone* is my rock" (v. 2), "Find rest, O my soul, in God *alone*" (v. 5), and "He *alone* is my rock" (v. 6). But in verse 4 the translators thought they needed to use the word *fully* ("They *fully* intend to topple him"), and in verse 9 they use the pale word *but* ("Lowborn men are *but* a breath").

Marvin Tate makes a stab at a more reflective rendering by using the word *yes*:

> Yes, my soul waits calmly for God . . .
> Yes, he is my rock where I am secure . . .
> Yes, despite being a person of high status . . .
> Yes, calmly wait for God, O my soul . . .
> Yes, he is my rock where I am secure . . .
> Yes, ordinary people are only a breath . . . [3]

Tate's effort captures something of the poem's style, but it misses the psalmist's emphasis upon God being his *only* object of faith and trust, which is the most important thing. As I said, it is almost impossible to capture the full force of the original in our translations.

But let me repeat this: The most important thing about Psalm 62 is that the psalmist is making God his *only* object of trust. He is not trusting something other than God, nor is he trusting God and something else, or God and someone else. His trust is in God only. God is worthy of his trust, and that is why David is so confident.

Alexander Maclaren, one of the best of all commentators and preachers on the psalms, captures this when he says, "That one word [*only*] is the record of conflict and the trophy of [the psalmist's] victory."[4]

◌ **Psalm 62** ◌

I think this is something Christians in our day especially need to learn. As I see it, our problem is not that we do not trust God, at least in some sense. We have to do that to be Christians. To become a Christian you have to trust God in the matter of salvation at least. It is rather that we do not trust God *only*, meaning that we always want to add something else to trust as well.

I think this is what was disturbing John MacArthur when he wrote the book *Our Sufficiency in Christ.*[5] Quite a few people did not like that book, because it was a critique of the way many of today's Christians depend on mystical experiences, pragmatic solutions to problems, and psychology rather than fully trusting Christ for guidance, help, and wholeness, and the critics wanted to argue for a proper use of these experiences, methodologies, and tools. They had their point, of course, because there is a legitimate place for experience, pragmatism, and professional counseling help, just as there is a legitimate place for doctors even though God is the ultimate source of bodily healing. Nevertheless, when I read the book I felt myself siding more with John MacArthur than with his critics. For I am a pastor too, as he is, and I too find that Christians in our day are far more inclined to trust the world's tools and mechanisms than to trust Jesus Christ wholly. For many of today's believers Jesus really is not sufficient for all things, regardless of what they may profess publicly.

Not long ago I was interviewed by a staff writer from *Christianity Today* about the impact of culture on the ministry, and I said that television has turned our age into an entertainment-oriented culture and that preachers therefore increasingly try to be entertainers. I explained how many churches have almost eliminated prayer from their services, substituted brainless music for the great theological hymns, and reduced the content of most sermons to a series of need-defining comments, trivial "teaching" lines, and funny anecdotes. The person interviewing me did not necessarily disagree, but he wondered what I would say to the argument that you have to begin where people are and that if people want entertainment, you have to provide it in order to have them listen.

I answered in two ways. I said that the simplest response, a simplistic answer but one that nevertheless has some truth in it, is that of course that is true. You do have to begin where people are. Moreover, I said, anyone who is any good at communicating does that, even those who are determined to teach the Word of God. People have to be trained to listen. And like any other subject, you have to master the ABCs of biblical content and theology before you can go on to higher and more complicated matters.

But, I said, there is also another answer, and in my opinion it is here that the real problem lies. The real problem is a crisis of faith, lack of belief in God and the power of the Word of God. The real reason preachers do not teach the Bible and resort to other devices such as "lite" theology and funny stories is that they do not trust God. They do not believe that God actually works through his Word to convert unbelievers and strengthen and form character in Christians. They do not believe that God reveals his will sufficiently through the Bible. They do not believe that faithful Bible teaching will transform individuals and rejuvenate society. I think John MacArthur is aware of this and has been dismayed by the current drift of evangelical Christianity too, which is why he wrote *Our Sufficiency in Christ*.

But doesn't "felt-need" preaching work, someone will ask. Doesn't entertainment fill churches? Well, yes, when it is well done it often does fill churches. If you give people what they want, they will come for it. But this is not the same thing as serving Jesus as one of his undershepherds or doing kingdom

∽ Psalm 62 ∾

work. It is merely doing the world's work in the world's way. Moreover, it is a betrayal of God. For, as Bible teacher John Trapp said, "They trust not God *at all* who trust not him *alone*."[6]

To pretend to trust God but not to trust him only is like having one foot on a solid foundation and the other on an object that is unstable and is moving away from the foundation. When I was a teenager my family had a cottage on a lake in New York State, and my grandmother, who was a very heavy woman, came to visit us in the summer. On one of these visits my father took her out in our motorboat. After the ride he returned to the dock and began to help my grandmother out of the boat. Unfortunately, he had not tied the boat to the dock. So as soon as she had one foot on the dock her weight began to push the boat away from it, and with one foot on the dock and the other on the boat, and with no way to stop the boat from drifting, she slowly sank down between the dock and boat and splashed into the water.

That is what will happen to you if you try to trust God *and something else*. You will find that you are actually not trusting God at all and that you will fall. David did not make that mistake. He had learned that if he was to trust God at all, he had to trust him only, and when he did, he found that God was indeed his "rock," his "salvation," and his "fortress." Fixed on that rock, David knew that he would "never be shaken," as he says in verse 2.

Still Will We Trust

Still, David had to keep trusting, and he knew how variable and weak the faith of man in God can be. This is emphasized in the second stanza. David had trusted God. But now he also

(1) encourages himself to continue to trust God (vv. 5–7) and (2) urges the people to trust God too (v. 8).

There is a great deal of similarity between the first and second stanzas of this psalm, because the first two verses are repeated again as verses 5 and 6, which begin stanza two. They are not a refrain (like the refrains in Psalms 57 and 59) but rather a thematic statement that repeats the necessity for trusting God alone. They are repeated because this is what the psalm is emphasizing.

There is a slight change the second time around, however. In the first occurrence David declared that he did trust God and that he had found rest in him. In the second stanza he urges himself to find rest in God and to continue in it. How does he do this? Well, in the first case, after he had expressed trust in God alone, he looked aside to reflect on the evil of those surrounding him, the people who were trying to knock him over like a tottering wall. In this second instance, where he is encouraging himself to continue to trust God, he does not think about his enemies but rather focuses on God instead.

How does he focus on God? He does it by repeating in verse 7 the images he has used to describe God in verses 2 and 6, bringing them before his mind once again. He says in verse 7:

> My salvation and my honor depend on God;
>   he is my mighty rock, my refuge.

Salvation, rock, and refuge (or fortress) were mentioned in verse 6, just one verse before.

Here is a point where we can all learn from David. Alexander Maclaren preached a sermon in which he compared verses 1 and 5, pointing out that although the settled confidence that David shows in verse 1 may be beyond us, his desire to find rest in God is nevertheless something we can copy. Maclaren said, "This man's profession of utter resignation is perhaps too high for us; but we can make his *self-exhortation* our own."[7] That is exactly right, and, of course, that is precisely what he urges on the people in verse 8: "Trust in him at all times, O people; pour out your hearts to him, for God is our refuge."

A New Look at Weak Man

If we are to divide the psalm into three stanzas, marked by the *selah*s at the end of verses 4 and 8, then the last stanza (vv. 9–12) echoes the first in that each is about both God and man. The first is about God and David's enemies, in that order. The third is about mankind in general and God; the matter is the same but the order is reversed.

Yet there is a big difference the second time around. David is thinking about his enemies again in this stanza, but in the meantime he has settled himself on God, and as a result his focus has changed significantly.

I mentioned three interacting agents in stanza one: God, the psalmist, and the psalmist's enemies. Those agents are also here (the presence of the psalmist is implied). But in the earlier stanza David was looking at his enemies in relationship to himself, and he was primarily aware of the danger he was in. They were about to push him over like a tottering wall. Here he is looking at his enemies in relationship to God, whom he has continued to trust (particularly in stanza two), and by that comparison he sees that these supposedly dangerous men are "only a breath." They are not worth fearing. In fact, "If weighed on [this] balance, they are nothing" (v. 9).

Derek Kidner suggests that there are two important points here: (1) We have nothing to fear from man, and (2) we have nothing to hope from man, either.[8] These are both true, and both flow out of the lessons the psalm as a whole has been teaching.

Most of us who are Christians are willing to agree—at least in our speech—that we do not have to fear man. We believe that Jesus is strong and that God is able to care for us. We find the words "Surely I am with you always, to the very end of the age" to be a great comfort (Matt. 28:20). It is the second part we have trouble with. We trust God, but we want to trust man too, or at least look to other people for something we doubt God is able or willing to supply. But other people will always let us down. They are sinners, as we are. They cannot be trusted. But even if they could be, they are still "but a breath" and are quickly taken away and are gone. If God has given you faithful and good friends or a loving life companion, thank him for it. These are great gifts. But do not place your deepest hope in man. Instead, trust him who is eternal and unchanging, and you will never be shaken when people disappoint you.

Two Lessons Learned about God

The last two verses of Psalm 62 are intended as a summary of what David has been learning, but they also go a step beyond it. David says that he has learned two lessons: God is strong and God is loving.

The opening lines of verse 11 ("One thing God has spoken, two things have I heard") can be taken in three ways. First, they can mean that God has spoken one thing twice. That is, God has repeated his lesson for emphasis. Second, they can mean that God has taught David two lessons, *one* and *two* being only a Semitic literary device. Third, they can mean that God spoke once but that David learned two things from it. Probably what these words intend is that David has learned two great things about God as a result of God's continuing self-revelation of himself.

First, God is strong: He is sovereign in all the events of history, including the dangers that have threatened David. Second, God is loving and merciful, even in these apparently contradictory things. The word David uses is *hesed,* which always refers to God's faithful covenants with his people. It means that he is a covenant-keeping God.

If you know anything about God and the salvation he has provided for you in Jesus Christ, you should be rejoicing in these two great attributes of God also, as David did. There would be no salvation for you or anyone else if God lacked either. If God had power but lacked mercy, he would have been able to save mankind, but he would have had no inclination to do so. If God was merciful but lacked power, he might have desired to save us, but he would not have been able to do it. Fortunately, God is both all-powerful and compassionate. Therefore, he has reached out to save us and has been successful in doing so through Jesus Christ.

J. J. Stewart Perowne reflects on these attributes in a slightly broader way, saying, "This is the only truly worthy representation of God. Power without love is brutality, and love without power is weakness. Power is the strong foundation of love, and love is the beauty and the crown of power."[9] This is why we can also "rest in God alone." We can come to God for help because he loves us and invites us to come to him. Once there, we can rest in perfect contentment, because we know that God is also able to protect us. Indeed, he is more than able. He is an impregnable fortress.

Psalm 63

O God, you are my God,
  earnestly I seek you;
my soul thirsts for you,
  my body longs for you,
in a dry and weary land
  where there is no water.

I have seen you in the sanctuary
  and beheld your power and your glory.
Because your love is better than life,
  my lips will glorify you.
I will praise you as long as I live,
  and in your name I will lift up my hands.
My soul will be satisfied as with the richest of foods;
  with singing lips my mouth will praise you.

On my bed I remember you;
  I think of you through the watches of the night.
Because you are my help,
  I sing in the shadow of your wings.
My soul clings to you;
  your right hand upholds me.

They who seek my life will be destroyed;
  they will go down to the depths of the earth.

They will be given over to the sword
   and become food for jackals.

But the king will rejoice in God;
   all who swear by God's name will praise him,
   while the mouths of liars will be silenced.

A Love Better Than Life

There are three types of people in any Christian gathering. There are those who are followers of Jesus Christ in name only, which means that they are Christians in name only. They seem to be following after God and Christ and say they are, but theirs is a false following, like that of the five foolish virgins who did not truly know the Lord and were rejected by him. The second class are those who are following Jesus but are following at a distance, like Peter was at the time of Jesus' arrest. The third type are those who, as Murdoch Campbell suggests, "in storm and sunshine, cleave to him and enjoy daily communion with him."[1] These people want God, and they want him intensely, because they know that he and he alone will satisfy the deep longing of their souls.

David was a person who desired God above everything else. He had faults, but desire for God was a wonderful characteristic of David that we see throughout his long life. Psalm 63 is a classic expression of his longing and a good psalm with which to end these studies.

The Setting of the Psalm

The title of Psalm 63 identifies it as "a psalm of David" and indicates that it was written "when he was in the Desert of

161

Judah." There are only two periods in David's life this can apply to: (1) when he was in the wilderness early in his life fleeing from King Saul or (2) later when he was in the wilderness fleeing from his son Absalom. The second must be the case here, because in verse 11 David refers to himself as "the king," and he was not yet king when he was fleeing from King Saul.

The story of Absalom's rebellion is told in 2 Samuel 15–19. Absalom was estranged from his father because he felt that David had mistreated him. He spent four years doing his utmost to win over the hearts of the people of Israel, and when he thought he was ready he set up a rival kingship in the nearby city of Hebron. Caught off guard, David feared an attack on Jerusalem and fled the city with those who remained loyal to him. Wise military strategists recommended that Absalom attack David at once, while he was still off balance and unable to resist an assault, but God caused Absalom to listen to counselors who advised delay, and by the time the battle finally came, David was ready and Absalom's army was soundly defeated by David's battle-seasoned soldiers led by his faithful general, Joab. Twenty thousand men perished in that battle, and Absalom was one of them. He was caught in a tree while fleeing on a mule and was slain by Joab.

This historical setting throws light on some of the psalm's expressions: "better than life," "as long as I live," and "they who seek my life," for instance (vv. 3, 4, 9). They remind us that David was literally in danger of death at Absalom's hand. The setting also gives added weight to David's description of himself as "the king," reminding everyone that he was the true king as opposed to the pretender.

The setting also helps us appreciate the emotional passion of the psalm. Separated from God's sanctuary, which was in Jerusalem and which David loved, David is longing for a sense of the presence of God as a friend longs for one from whom he is separated or as a lover longs for his or her beloved. This makes the psalm almost a love song for God, especially when David says, "My soul thirsts for you, my body longs for you" (v. 1). Commentator Derek Kidner says, "There may be other songs that equal this outpouring of devotion; [but there are] few if any that surpass it."[2] J. J. Stewart Perowne wrote, "This is unquestionably one of the most beautiful and touching psalms in the whole Psalter."[3]

The longing for God expressed here is similar to that in some of the psalms of the sons of Korah, especially Psalms 42, 43, and 84. Psalm 63 is also similar in tone to Psalms 61, 62, and 64, which indicates that the historical setting of those psalms might also be the period in which David fled from Absalom.

Longing for God

Commentators have suggested various ways of outlining the eleven verses of this psalm. The New International Version is probably right on track, however, when it sets verse 1 off as a stanza to itself. It expresses the longing of David's soul for God. The next section (vv. 2–8) describes how that longing has been answered in the past and is being honored in the present.

Verse 1 is a wonderful expression of the very heart of religion. David is in the Desert of Judah, one of the most barren regions on earth, and he uses that as a poetic background for his condition apart from God. He has been driven from Jerusalem, where God was present in his sanctuary and where he regularly worshiped and beheld God's glory. He therefore sees himself now as thirsting for God as a man might thirst in the desert, "where there is no water," and as longing physically for God as a traveler through such hostile country might long for rest at the end of his debilitating journey.

This intense physical longing for God, almost an appetite for God, is something that impressed C. S. Lewis when he was preparing his *Reflections on the Psalms*. He wrote, "These poets knew far less reason than we for loving God. They did not know that he offered them eternal joy; still less that he would die to win it for them. Yet they express a longing for him, for his mere presence, which comes only to the best Christians or to Christians in their best moments. They long to live all their days in the temple so that they may constantly see 'the fair beauty of the Lord' (Ps. 27:4). Their longing to go up to Jerusalem and 'appear before the presence of God' is like a physical thirst (Ps. 42). From Jerusalem his presence flashes out 'in perfect beauty' (Ps. 50:2). Lacking that encounter with him, their souls are parched like a waterless countryside (Ps. 63:1)."[4]

How little this is found today! Most people do not even know that it is God their souls truly desire. They are seeking satisfaction in things. Others know God but do not cultivate his presence; they do not long after him. Is it not this above everything that explains the weakness of the contemporary church? Is it not this that makes us so hollow spiritually? In my judgment, it needs to be said of many of today's Christians that they have a form of religion but without its power, because they do not deeply know or deeply desire God.

One other thing is worth noting about verse 1. The verb *seek* is an unusual verb that is related to the Hebrew noun for *dawn*, and it can be translated two ways, either as "to seek early" or "to seek earnestly." The New International Version has chosen the second option ("earnestly I seek you"), probably rightly, but many of the older versions, including the King James Version, used "early." This caused Christians to think of Psalm 63 as a morning psalm, and in many places it was sung at the beginning of each day. For example, it was used as a morning psalm by the early Greek churches and it remains such in the liturgy of the Armenian church.

Liturgy aside, however, the point is the desirability of a regular, early, daily longing after God. Do you have that desire for God? Do you want it? Are you willing to develop it? There is no better way to start each day than by earnestly seeking God's face through personal Bible study, meditation, and devout prayer.

Satisfaction in God

About a thousand years after these words were written, David's greater descendant, Jesus Christ, said, "Ask and it will be given to you; seek and you will find; knock and the door will be opened to you" (Matt. 7:7). David did not know these specific words, of course. But he did know the reality of them and elaborates on this idea in the next section (verses 2–8).

There are various ways these verses can be studied. For example, they might be outlined as God's past, present, and future satisfying of David. *The past:* "I have seen you in the sanctuary and beheld your power and your glory" (v. 2). It is the memory of those joyous moments that makes David's present circumstances painful. *The present:* "Your love is better than life" (v. 3), "On my bed I remember you; I think of you through the watches of the night" (v. 6), "You are my help" (v. 7), "Your right hand upholds me" (v. 8). Even though he is cut off from the sanctuary in Jerusalem, God has not cut himself off from David. As Spurgeon said, "There was no desert in his heart, though there was a desert around him."[5] *The future:* "My soul will be satisfied as with the richest of foods; with singing lips my mouth will praise you" (v. 5). Because God is the same and does not change, the one who has found God able to satisfy his longings in the past can know that he will continue to satisfy him completely in the present and in the future too.

If we outline the verses in this way, they become a means of exploring God's character and stressing his inexhaustible capacity for satisfying our deepest spiritual desires. They are a development of Saint Augustine's well-known words: "Our hearts are restless till they find rest in thee."[6]

Again, this section can be studied for how David praises God. Commentator Thomas Le Blanc saw David doing this in seven ways (based on the King James Version):

> First, he [David] extols the loving-kindness of God with *his lips* (v. 3): "My lips shall praise thee." Secondly, with *his tongue* (v. 4): "Thus will I bless thee while I live." Thirdly, with *his hands:* "I will lift up my hands in thy name." Fourthly, with *his will* (v. 5): "My soul shall be satisfied as with marrow and fatness." Fifthly, with *his mouth:* "And my mouth shall praise thee with joyful lips." Sixthly, with *his memory* (v. 6): "When I remember thee upon my bed." Seventhly and lastly, with *his intellect:* "And meditate on thee in the night watches."[7]

If we handle the verses in this way, they become a means of exploring what it means to be a human being and how each part of a person's physical and emotional makeup can be used to praise God. Most people use only about a tenth of their brain, and it would be highly worthwhile to find out how to use just a few percentage points more of our mental capacities. In the same way, it would be worthwhile to find out how to use just a bit more of our potential capacity for praising God.

But let me suggest another way of looking at this section of the psalm. We can see it as statements, first, of David's satisfaction in God, and then, of two results flowing from it.

◌◌ **Psalm 63** ◌◌

1. *David is satisfied with, in, and by God.* This is the main point
of what he is saying, and it flows from his opening expression
of deep longing. David longs for God, and therefore David is
satisfied with God. God does not hold himself back from those
who seek him. Rather he gives himself to them fully and in
increasingly fuller ways. That is why David can speak of past,
present, and future satisfaction.

It is also why he speaks of God's love being "better than
life" (v. 3). This verse contains two things, each of which is
acknowledged as good, and it compares them, concluding that
the loving-kindness of God is best. Everyone acknowledges
that life is good. Therefore most of us try to hang on to life at
whatever cost. We will give up our money rather than be shot
by a thief who wants our wallet. We will submit to painful sur-
gical procedures or even to amputations of a limb if those
things will restore us to even partial health and prolong our
days. Satan used this truth to slander righteous Job, declar-
ing, "Skin for skin! A man will give all he has for his own life"
(Job 2:4). For nearly everyone, life is the most precious of all
possessions.

However, says David, there is something even better than
life, and that is the love of God. The word he uses is *hesed*,
which is often translated as loving-kindness or covenant love.
It stresses the faithful continuance of God's love. God's love
is steady and unchangeable, which is why it is better than even
the best thing in life, which is life itself. Life can be lost, even
though we value it and try to protect it at all costs. But the
covenant love of God can never be lost. The apostle Paul asked,
"Who shall separate us from the love of Christ? Shall trouble
or hardship or persecution or famine or nakedness or danger
or sword?" (Rom. 8:35). He answered, "No, in all these things
we are more than conquerors through him who loved us. For
I am convinced that neither death nor life, neither angels nor

demons, neither the present nor the future, nor any powers, neither height nor depth, nor anything else in all creation, will be able to separate us from the love of God that is in Christ Jesus our Lord" (Rom. 8:37–39).

In view of such great love, isn't it strange that we spend so much time trying to find satisfaction elsewhere, even in earthly loves, and so little time seeking and enjoying the lasting love of God?

When I remember that David wrote earlier in the psalm about seeking God as a thirsty man seeks water, I think of a fountain on Sedgley Hill in Philadelphia, where I live. If a person makes his way out along the eastern side of the Schuylkill River, he will come to the statue of a pilgrim where a small spring empties into the river. Then, if he follows the course of that stream upward onto the hill, he will come to a spring, which is its source, and he will see an inscription erected there years ago by the government of the city. It reads: "Whosoever drinketh of this water shall thirst again," a quotation from Jesus' conversation with the woman of Samaria (John 4:13 KJV).

That quotation tells us that all earthly satisfactions ultimately are unsatisfying, just because they are earthly. They are not eternal; we are beings made for eternity. But Jesus went on to say what the city fathers of Philadelphia did not acknowledge, "But whoever drinks the water I give him will never thirst. Indeed, the water I give him will become in him a spring of water welling up to eternal life" (John 4:14).

David had drunk of the spring of the covenant love of God, and he was forever satisfied. And so shall we be!

2. *As a first result of being satisfied by the eternal loving-kindness of God, David praises God.* David was so abundantly satisfied with the love of God that he wanted everyone else to know about God's love too.

෴ Psalm 63 ෴

In the days of Elisha the armies of Ben-Haded, the king of Aram, were besieging Samaria, and God scattered them by causing them to hear the sound of chariots, horses, and a great army so that they panicked and fled, leaving their tents and provisions behind and their arms and other valuables strewn over the route they fled by. There were about forty lepers at the entrance of Samaria's city gate. They decided to go to the camp of the enemy soldiers to get some food from them, because the lepers, like the shut-up citizens of Samaria, were starving. When they arrived in the camp they discovered that it was deserted. So they had a great time. They ate and drank and took the silver and gold and costly clothing and carried it off and hid it. Then they came back and took more.

At last they came to their senses and said, "We're not doing right. This is a day of good news and we are keeping it to ourselves. If we wait until daylight [that is, until tomorrow], punishment will overtake us. Let's go at once and report this to the royal palace" (2 Kings 7:9). They did, and by nightfall sacks of flour and barley, nearly nonexistent just a day before, were being sold for pennies in the market.

The point is that it is both natural and right to share good news. David knew this, and his song of unmixed praise of the God who satisfies our deepest longings is the result. Verse 3 says, "*Because* your love is better than life, my lips will glorify you," and verse 7 makes the same connection: "*Because* you are my help, I sing in the shadow of your wings." It is because of who God is that we praise him. It is because of his faithful helping of us in trouble that we sing his praises.

John Donne, the great English metaphysical poet who later became a preacher of the gospel, wrote of verse 7 that "as the spirit and soul of the whole book of Psalms is contracted into this psalm, so is the spirit and soul of the whole psalm contracted into this verse."[8] He meant that the Psalter shows how the person who has found satisfaction in God sings about it. Of course, Donne did that himself in his religious poetry.

3. *As a second result of being satisfied by the great loving-kindness of God, David wants to stay close to God.* This too is a natural consequence of being deeply satisfied. Verse 8 says, "My soul clings to you." In Hebrew this is actually "cleaves to you," a phrase that is used for the attachment between a husband and wife or of other tight relationships, such as Ruth's attachment to her mother-in-law, Naomi (Ruth 1:14). If you have been satisfied by God, isn't it true that you will want to stay close to him too? If you are not cleaving to him, perhaps it is because you have never sought him enough to be truly and deeply satisfied.

Vindication by God

The last three verses of the psalm look to the future and express David's confidence that in time his enemies will be destroyed, the mouths of those who have slandered him will be silenced, and he will again be openly praising God with others who also love and seek him.

Pedantic commentators feel that these last verses are an unworthy blemish upon what was otherwise a particularly beautiful psalm, and some have suggested that they were tacked on later by a somewhat insensitive editor. This is not the case at all. They simply bring us back to where we started, in the desert with David, and they remind us that this is a real world after all and that, if we are to be genuinely satisfied with God's love, it must not be in some never-never land but right here in the midst of this world's disappointments, frustrations, and dangers. In other words, it is at the very time when his son had betrayed him and was seeking to kill him that David found the Lord's love to be richly satisfying.

꩜ **Psalm 63** ꩜

Given these circumstances, the psalm is an amazing triumph of faith, as so many of David's psalms are, especially those from these dark periods of his life. But, as G. Campbell Morgan writes, "Two things are necessary for such triumph as this. These are indicated in the opening words of the psalm. First, there must be the consciousness of personal relationship, 'O God, Thou art my God'; and secondly, there must be earnest seeking after God, 'Early will I seek Thee.'"[9] Because that is true, a wise man or woman will pursue these goals carefully. Will you?

Notes

Psalm 52: Righteous Judgment for a Wicked Man

1. Derek Kidner, *Psalms 1–72: An Introduction and Commentary on Books I and II of the Psalms* (Downers Grove, Ill.: InterVarsity Press, 1973), 195.

2. C. H. Spurgeon, *The Treasury of David,* vol. 1b, *Psalms 27–57* (Grand Rapids: Zondervan Publishing House, 1968), 428.

Psalm 53: A Psalm That Is Repeated

1. Spurgeon, *The Treasury of David,* vol. 1b, 433.

2. Matthew Henry, *Commentary on the Whole Bible,* vol. 3, *Job to Song of Solomon* (Grand Rapids: Fleming H. Revell, n.d.), 439.

3. Henry, *Commentary on the Whole Bible,* vol. 3, 439.

Psalm 54: Betrayed

1. Kidner, *Psalms 1–72,* 197.

2. A. Weiser, *The Psalms: A Commentary,* trans. H. Hartwell (Philadelphia: The Westminster Press, 1962), cited by Marvin E. Tate, *Word Biblical Commentary,* vol. 20, *Psalms 51–100* (Dallas: Word Publishing, 1990), 49.

3. Spurgeon, *The Treasury of David,* vol. 1b, 442.

Psalm 55: Betrayed by a Close Friend

1. G. Campbell Morgan, *Notes on the Psalms* (Grand Rapids: Fleming H. Revell, 1947), 101–2. See also J. J. Stewart Perowne, *Commentary on the Psalms* (Grand Rapids: Kregel Publications, 1989; original edition 1878–79), vol. 1, 436; H. C. Leupold, *Exposition of the Psalms* (Grand Rapids: Baker Book House, 1969), 420–25; and Alexander Maclaren, *The Psalms,* vol. 2, *Psalms 39–89* in The Expositor's Bible series, ed. W. Robertson Nicoll (New York: A. C. Armstrong and Son, 1893), 159–70.

2. Tate, *Word Biblical Commentary,* vol. 20, 56.

3. Spurgeon is the only major commentator who has an outline similar to this. See *The Treasury of David,* vol. 1b, 445.

4. Spurgeon, *The Treasury of David,* vol. 1b, 448.

5. Perowne, *Commentary on the Psalms,* vol. 1, 439.

Psalm 56: "What Can Man Do to Me?"

1. Kidner, *Psalms 1–72,* 202.

2. Perowne, *Commentary on the Psalms,* vol. 1, 444. This psalm is one of two that flowered from this crisis. The other is Psalm 34.

3. Alexander Maclaren, *Expositions of Holy Scripture,* vol. 3, *The Psalms, Isaiah 1–48* (Grand Rapids: Wm. B. Eerdmans, 1959), 46.

Psalm 57: Hiding in Thee

1. There are two caves to which the heading of Psalm 57 could refer: (1) the cave of Adullam (1 Sam. 22:1), and (2) the cave at En Gedi (1 Sam. 24:1–22). It is probably the first because of the obvious connection of this with the preceding psalm.

2. H. C. Leupold, *Exposition of the Psalms* (Grand Rapids: Baker Book House, 1969), 431. See also Perowne, *Commentary on the Psalms,* vol. 1, 450–51. Psalms 56 and 59 also have a repeated refrain and can be outlined similarly.

3. For a good listing see Franz Delitzsch, *Biblical Commentary on the Psalms,* vol. 2, ed. Francis Bolton (Grand Rapids: Wm. B. Eerdmans, n.d.), 173.

4. Kidner, *Psalms 1–72,* 206.

5. Maclaren, *Expositions of Holy Scripture,* vol. 3, 48–49.

Psalm 58: Low Deeds in High Places

1. Quoted by Charles W. Colson in "The Problem of Ethics," a speech delivered to students at the Harvard Business School and published by the Wilberforce Forum, a division of Prison Fellowship (Washington: The Wilberforce Forum, 1992), 5.

2. Colson, "The Problem of Ethics," 3–4.

3. Perowne, *Commentary on the Psalms,* vol. 1, 454.

4. Perowne, *Commentary on the Psalms,* vol. 1, 455.

5. Maclaren, *The Psalms,* vol. 2, 194.

6. For a complete discussion of these options and a balanced suggestion of a good translation see Perowne, *Commentary on the Psalms,* vol. 1, 459. Maclaren is also helpful. See *The Psalms,* vol. 2, 194–96.

7. Maclaren, *The Psalms,* vol. 2, 195.

8. Quoted in C. H. Spurgeon, *The Treasury of David,* vol. 2a, *Psalms 58–87* (Grand Rapids: Zondervan Publishing House, 1968), 4.

9. Colson, "The Problem of Ethics," 22–23.

Psalm 59: God Is My Fortress

1. Tate has an interesting list of word parallels between this psalm and 1 Samuel 19 and 24, which also suggests a connection between the psalm and the historical setting: *watch* (v. 9), *morning* (v. 16), *innocence* (vv. 3–4), *seeing* (vv. 4, 10), *dogs* (vv. 6, 7, 14, 15), *ambush* (v. 3), and *blood* (v. 2). See Tate, *Word Biblical Commentary,* vol. 20, 95.

2. See Kidner, *Psalms 1–72,* 211.

3. Tate, *Word Biblical Commentary,* vol. 20, 99.

4. Leupold, *Exposition of the Psalms,* 443.

5. Albert Smith, *A Month at Constantinople,* quoted by C. H. Spurgeon, *The Treasury of David,* vol. 2a, 20.

6. Maclaren, *Expositions of Holy Scripture,* vol. 3, 61.

Psalm 60: If God Does Not Go with Us

1. Marvin Tate says that Aram Naharaim is a name for Mesopotamia and that Aram Zobah "refers to a major Aramean state during the time of David, located on the eastern slopes of the Anti-Lebanon mountain range in the Biqa Valley" (Tate, *Word Biblical Commentary,* vol. 20, 104–5).

2. Kidner, *Psalms 1–72,* 215.

3. A parallel account appears in 1 Chronicles 18:1–13.

4. First Chronicles 18:12 credits the slaying of the eighteen thousand to Abishai, another of David's commanders. He could have been a commander under David during the follow-up campaign.

5. Spurgeon, *The Treasury of David,* vol. 2a, 27.

6. The first part of Psalm 108 is adapted from Psalm 57:7–11.

7. For a helpful study of these place names and their significance see Leupold, *Exposition of the Psalms,* 450–51, and Perowne, *Commentary on the Psalms,* vol. 1, 472–73.

8. Leupold, *Exposition of the Psalms,* 448.

9. Leupold, *Exposition of the Psalms,* 452.

Psalm 61: The Rock That Is Higher Than I

1. See Franz Delitzsch, *Biblical Commentary on the Psalms,* trans. Francis Bolton (Grand Rapids: Wm. B. Eerdmans, n.d.), vol. 2, 202; Perowne, *Commentary on the Psalms,* vol. 1, 478; Kidner, *Psalms 1–72,* 218–20.

2. Leupold, *Exposition of the Psalms,* 458.

3. Maclaren, *The Psalms,* vol. 2, 217–18.

4. Tate, *Word Biblical Commentary,* vol. 20, 116.

5. See Psalms 18:2, 31, 46; 19:14; 28:1; 31:2–3; 40:2; 61:2; 62:2, 6–7; 71:3; 78:35; 89:26; 92:15; 94:22; 95:1; 144:1.

6. Spurgeon, *The Treasury of David,* vol. 2a, 40.

7. See also Psalms 15:1; 23:6; 43:3; 84:4. Franz Delitzsch writes, "During the time the tabernacle was still being moved from place to place we hear no such mention of dwelling in God's tabernacle or house. It was David who coined this expression for loving fellowship with the God of revelation, simultaneously with his preparation of a settled dwelling-place for the sacred Ark." See Delitzsch, *Biblical Commentary on the Psalms,* vol. 2, 203.

8. Quoted in Spurgeon, *The Treasury of David,* vol. 2a, 46.

Psalm 62: Rest in God Alone

1. Leupold, *Exposition of the Psalms,* 458.

2. Perowne, *Commentary on the Psalms,* vol. 1, 480.

3. Tate, *Word Biblical Commentary,* vol. 20, 117.

4. Maclaren, *Expositions of Holy Scripture,* vol. 3, 67.

5. John MacArthur, Jr., *Our Sufficiency in Christ* (Dallas, Word Publishing, 1991).

6. Quoted in Spurgeon, *The Treasury of David,* vol. 2a, 55.

7. Maclaren, *Expositions of Holy Scripture,* vol. 3, 70.

8. Kidner, *Psalms 1–72,* 223.

9. Perowne, *Commentary on the Psalms,* vol. 1, 484.

Psalm 63: A Love Better Than Life

1. Murdoch Campbell, *From Grace to Glory: Meditations on the Book of Psalms* (Carlisle, Pa.: Banner of Truth Trust, 1970), 109.

2. Kidner, *Psalms 1–72,* 224.

3. Perowne, *Commentary on the Psalms,* vol. 1, 486.

4. C. S. Lewis, *Reflections on the Psalms* (New York: Harcourt, Brace and Company, 1958), 50–51.

5. Spurgeon, *The Treasury of David,* vol. 2a, 65.

6. Augustine, *The Confessions,* Book I, paragraph 1, in *Basic Writings of Saint Augustine,* ed. Whitney J. Oates (New York: Random House, 1948), vol. 1, 3.

7. Quoted in Spurgeon, *The Treasury of David,* vol. 2a, 73.

8. John Donne, *Sermon 66,* quoted in Perowne, *Commentary on the Psalms,* vol. 1, 489.

9. G. Campbell Morgan, *Notes on the Psalms* (Grand Rapids: Fleming H. Revell, 1947), 112.